THE GIFT
of a
GOOD DEATH

Our palliative dementia story

Lisa Twigg

First published in Australia in 2024 by Lisa Twigg

Email for correspondence: lisa@eightyyearswithoutdementia.com
Website: https://www.lisatwigg.com

ISBN 9781763661806 (paperback)
ISBN 9781763661813 (ebook)

A catalogue record for this book is available from the National Library of Australia

Disclaimer

The material in this publication is of the nature of general comment only, and does not represent professional advice. To the maximum extent permitted by law, the author and publisher disclaim all responsibility and liability arising directly or indirectly from any person taking or not taking action based on the information in this publication.

Cover image: Photo of view from Dad's window

Foreword

Having read Lisa's first book and heard her family's story, I was keen to learn how Lisa, along with her family, was able to fulfill her dad's final wish to die at home.

I had heard about Lisa and her first book, *80 Years Without Dementia*, in December 2023, and finally met her in April 2024 at the Moreton Bay Dementia Alliance meeting. She spoke about her first book with raw honesty and passion. In sharing her dad's story, Lisa brings hope to other families who are in similar situations, showing them that there is almost always choice at the end of life.

Dementia is a terminal disease and, sadly, there is still no cure. As Lisa mentions in this book, there is a perception in the wider community that palliative care is for cancer patients or those with a well-recognised terminal illness. Provision of palliative care services for people who are living with dementia and are at the end-of-life stage is comparatively very low. This needs to change.

The Gift of a Good Death: Our Palliative Dementia Story is a beautiful read, relaying one family's journey during the final months of their loved one's life. It shows how the unconventional decision was made to bring him home, leaving the nursing home he had lived in for two years, to die surrounded by family in his home environment.

This story also gives practical tips for getting your affairs in order and how to start the conversation on what a good death looks like for someone diagnosed with dementia (or any terminal illness). What are your end-of-life wishes? Where would you like to die? Lisa encourages us to not be afraid and to talk about death and dying with our family. She emphasises again that palliative care services and support are available for people living with dementia.

Thank you to Lisa and her mum for sharing their raw emotions and personal experience in this book. Beautifully done.

Leah Keating, Dementia Doula
LK Dementia Doula Services

Contents

Introduction   1

Chapter 1   Setting the scene   5

Chapter 2   The first fall and the subsequent decline   11

Chapter 3   Getting our 'ducks in a row'   21

Chapter 4   A lot can happen in 12 days   29

Chapter 5   Coming home   43

Chapter 6   QUT Body Bequest Program   53

Chapter 7   Marking the occasion with love, laughter and memories   59

Chapter 8   Advance care planning and getting your affairs in order   63

Chapter 9   The personal, and professional, growth continues   75

Chapter 10   Mum's turn to speak   95

Conclusion   103

Acknowledgements   109

About the author   111

Introduction

How we got here

Last year, I published my first ever book – *80 Years Without Dementia: Diagnosis Doesn't Define Life* – all about the valuable life lessons I learnt from my dad's experience of dementia. The book was dedicated to him, and my motivation in writing it was twofold:

- to create a legacy for my beloved Dad
- to educate the wider community about reframing a dementia diagnosis from an 'absolute' negative to a 'potential' positive, in the hope of reducing fear and misunderstanding around the disease.

Since its launch in September 2023, I have enjoyed getting out and about to share our family story, promoting the book's message and meeting others whose lives have been touched by dementia. The feedback I've received suggests that the personal narrative of the book resonates with those who have read it, as do the authenticity and the vulnerability displayed on each page. Most importantly, readers have reported that the book has decreased their feelings of being alone on their own family journey through dementia, and that they have taken great comfort from that realisation. As a family, we feel honoured to have impacted other families in such a positive way.

Dad was still alive when the book was published, although we had witnessed a significant decline in his health during the preceding month. The reality of his impending death was starting to hit home. We knew our days with him were coming to an end and, not unexpectedly, he died peacefully in November – what we have termed a 'good death'. I had always assumed I would add an epilogue to the book after Dad's death to 'close off the story' that had unfolded in those pages. However, as I shared our experience with several friends and peers in the days and weeks after Dad died, I began to realise there was more to say than just providing an update. So, here we are …

What's my intention in writing this book?

Knowing time with Dad was becoming more and more precious, we made a family decision to take him out of his nursing home and bring him back to the security and familiarity of his home environment to see out his final days. We provided care for him ourselves, and he died peacefully with us around him. It was an unconventional choice to make, taking him out of the facility he had lived in for more than two years, but it was the right choice for us, including Dad. And that's really what this book is about – promoting choice at the end of life.

Place of death is an important consideration when it comes to planning your 'best-case scenario' for dying. We quickly realised that what we wanted to do – bring Dad home to die – was somewhat unusual, but nevertheless very 'doable'. We had the three things we needed to be able to make it work – capacity, willingness and time – and were motivated by our love for Dad. His death delivered immediate peace, primarily due to us being aware of his wishes and being able to carry them out for him.

Dying at home is not for everyone, but we believe other families may consider the pathway we took if they know it's an option. Regardless of whether they follow our lead or not, if we can inspire and educate others by sharing our experience, we will have achieved our purpose.

What to expect from this book?

This book takes up where the last one left off. It focusses on the final few months of Dad's life and is, just like my first book, presented as a personal narrative. It does not claim to have all the answers, and I do not profess to be an expert in dementia palliation. This is a family story from the heart; a book about lived experience.

Chapter 1 'sets the scene', introducing dementia, palliative care and the 'dying scene' in Australia, then the basics of our family story.

Chapters 2, 3 and 4 summarise the decline we witnessed in Dad's condition and what led us to bring him home to die. Chapter 5 describes his final days at home.

Chapter 6 focusses on the body bequest program Dad enrolled in, and Chapter 7 describes how this (positively) affected the ways in which we marked the occasion of his death.

Advance care planning and the role it played in our decision-making is the focus of Chapter 8. In Chapter 9, I touch on some of the most significant things I have learnt as I have traversed the palliative dementia path with Dad over the last few years.

I hand the final chapter of the book over to Mum, and she describes how the final few months of Dad's life felt for her. That's a powerful read, even for me.

To some extent, the writing of this book has been a form of therapy – processing the last few months of Dad's life and reflecting on the decisions we made and why we made them. But beyond any therapeutic benefit to me, I am highly motivated to share the final chapter in Dad's story in the hope it may:

- provide comfort to other families facing similar challenges
- kickstart conversations about death and dying, something we need to be doing more often

- empower others to make choices about palliative and end-of-life care that are good for them and good for their loved ones.

I hope you enjoy our story and take at least one thought away with you after reading it. It is an honour for me to share this book on behalf of our family.

ONE

Setting the scene

Before we jump into our family story and explore our palliative dementia journey, let's:

- define dementia
- look at its prevalence
- agree on what we mean by palliative care and end-of-life care
- look at the 'dying scene' in Australia
- briefly explore our family situation
- summarise where our family was at 101 days before Dad died – the point at which this book starts and, I believe, the point at which Dad's end-of-life journey really began.

What is dementia?

Dementia is an umbrella term for a group of diseases that affect memory, thinking and the ability to perform daily activities. You may be familiar with the most common disease, Alzheimer's, but there is also vascular, Lewy body, frontotemporal and many other types of dementia. There is no cure for dementia – it is a terminal illness with a trajectory of steady decline over a number of years. Dementia is most commonly diagnosed over the age of 65; however, not all people will be affected by dementia as they age.

Disease prevalence

Dementia is the *second* leading cause of death of *all* Australians, and the *leading* cause of death for Australian *women*. Provisional data suggests dementia will soon be the leading cause of death in Australia. In 2024, it is estimated that more than 421,000 Australians live with dementia. This figure is projected to increase to more than 812,500 by 2054.[1] Across the globe, more than 55 million people live with a diagnosis of dementia.[2]

What is palliative care?

Palliative care is not well understood in the wider community. Some of the misconceptions are that it:

- relates purely to specific illnesses/diseases (particularly cancer)
- is only the domain of specialists
- focusses solely on medical intervention
- addresses only the needs of the person concerned and not their carers and/or family members
- means people are about to die.

Palliative Care Australia defines palliative care as:

> person and family-centred care provided for a person with an active, progressive, advanced disease, who has little or no prospect of cure and who is expected to die, and for whom the primary goal is to optimise the quality of life. Palliative care helps people live their life as fully and as comfortably as possible when living with a life-limiting or terminal illness. Palliative care identifies and treats symptoms which may be physical, emotional, spiritual or social ... Palliative care is

---

1. https://www.dementia.org.au/about-dementia/dementia-facts-and-figures
2. https://www.who.int/news-room/fact-sheets/detail/dementia

a family-centred model of care, meaning that family and carers can receive practical and emotional support.[3]

In other words, in the absence of a cure for their condition, palliative care offers people a focus on symptom management, minimising suffering and discomfort and optimising their quality of life. This may include:

- the administration of medications
- emotional, social and spiritual support for the person with the illness, as well as their carers and family members
- goal setting and future planning
- information and advice.

Palliative care can be offered at home, in community palliative care facilities (sometimes referred to as hospices), in nursing homes or in specialist hospital units.

What is the difference between palliative care and end-of-life care?

Palliative care is much more than just dying and end-stage care; it can be delivered months, or even years, before a person dies. It often includes a period of bereavement support for their loved ones afterwards.

End-of-life care is really about the terminal phase: the last weeks and days of a person's life.

---

3. https://palliativecare.org.au/resource/what-is-palliative-care

What does palliative care look like for people living with dementia?

> Palliative care has a well-developed conceptual framework and evidence base when it comes to chronic disease but the notion of palliative care for people with dementia has traditionally received less attention. Consequently, in Australia, palliative care services for dementia are inconsistent in the way they are delivered, they lack equitable service provision, and services lack unified standards and accepted definitions. Improving palliative care for people with dementia therefore must be a policy priority, Australia-wide, across the different states and territories.[4]

Dementia is a terminal disease with no cure or prospect of recovery. While those living with dementia may not necessarily have complex medical needs that would warrant specialist palliative care services, like others with a terminal illness they should expect high-quality palliative and end-of-life care, regardless of whether they are cared for at home or in a residential aged care facility. As you will read in Chapter 9, it is widely discussed within the palliative care sector that specialist services won't be able to cope with the growing demand on them as our population ages and we live longer. We must continue to extend the reach of palliative care into general health services, and we must strive to support dementia patients better, particularly those wishing to remain at home, offering them the same excellent level of person-centred palliative and end-of-life care as we do others with a terminal illness.

---

4. Dementia Australia Paper Number 43 (prepared in collaboration with Palliative Care Australia), 2017

The 'dying scene' in Australia

Over 160,000 people die each year in Australia. When surveyed in the absence of ill health and pain – not during an emotionally charged time of sickness, new diagnosis or impending death – 90% of the general population indicate their preference would be to die at home. However, for a whole host of reasons (some of which include lack of in-home support, inadequate symptom control and ongoing emotional distress), at-home death rates in Australia sit between 4% and 14% across the country.[5] In other words, the vast majority of people die either in a nursing home or in hospital, with a smaller proportion dying in a hospice or a specialised palliative care unit.

Our family situation

Mum and Dad moved in with my husband, our two (as they were at the time) young children and me in 2012, into a granny flat under our family home. Dad was diagnosed with dementia at the beginning of 2018 at the age of 81. This had been a 'slow burn' over a period of five or six years as we noticed more and more changes in his capacity – not only with short-term memory loss, but also in terms of poor judgement, decreased ability to perform everyday tasks, issues with planning and so on. We made the agonising decision to transfer Dad to a nursing home (little more than a five-minute drive away) in 2021, when the stress of providing full-time care for him at home became too much for Mum. As you will read in Chapter 5, Dad died in November 2023 and Mum remains in their flat, independent and in good health.

---

5. https://www.abc.net.au/listen/programs/lifematters/have-you-talked-to-your-loved-one-about-their-end-of-life-choice/103545296

The few months leading up to Dad's death

In July 2023, I was putting the finishing touches on my first book, and Dad was 86 years old, soon to turn 87. He was still eating (slower and not as much as in previous times), he was still walking (slower and with a stick or sometimes a frame), he was still talking (though not always coherently) and he was still enjoying coming home for lunch or afternoon tea or going out of his nursing home for a walk, a coffee or an ice-cream. Although his gradual deterioration was obvious and consistent with his disease trajectory, we hadn't necessarily begun actively preparing for his death. Due to a higher risk of developing infections and a weakened immune system in the advanced stages of dementia, we all assumed there was a reasonable possibility pneumonia would be the likely cause of Dad's death, given he had chronic obstructive pulmonary disease, a history of chest infections and pneumonia, and had received treatment for asthma almost all his adult life.

As things turned out, it wasn't pneumonia that ended Dad's life. He simply died from the terminal illness he had been diagnosed with almost six years earlier – dementia.

TWO

The first fall and the subsequent decline

A suspected broken hip

Exactly 101 days before he died, on Sunday 20 August 2023, Dad had an unwitnessed fall at his nursing home. He was found on the floor around 5:30am, seemingly on his way to the bathroom, and there was immediate concern he may have broken a hip. My husband had returned from an overseas humanitarian mission eight days earlier, so he, the kids and I were away from home for a week, catching up on some quality family time. When I got the phone call at 6:30am that Dad was being assessed by paramedics and would be transferred to hospital, my heart sank, and his death suddenly felt very close. I quickly updated my husband about what had happened, rang Mum to tell her as much as I knew, threw some items in the car and headed down the motorway towards home. I spoke to my eldest brother on my way to collect Mum, and together we gathered our thoughts and recapped Dad's wishes:

- He did not want any interventions that would prolong his life if quality of life was no longer present.

- He did not want to be resuscitated if quality of life was no longer present.

What we knew about Dad's wishes was based on conversations we'd had with him over the years and reflected in the paperwork he had completed soon after his official dementia diagnosis in 2018. As worried as I was about the news we had received and how Dad would be when we saw him, I felt confident in making the decisions Mum and I would have to make when we reached the hospital. Both my brothers were due to visit from interstate in a few weeks' time, so discussions began on whether those visits may need to be brought forwards, dependent on what panned out as the day wore on.

When Mum and I arrived in a very busy, public emergency department that Sunday morning, Dad was peacefully asleep. This had not been the case earlier, however, and medical staff reported he had been agitated, combative and stressed during their initial examinations, requiring medication to settle. Their investigations to that point suggested his hip was not broken, given the range of movement he had; however, his behaviour was indicative of someone experiencing significant pain, although his dementia meant he was unable to accurately report this.

So began a long and extremely stressful hospital presentation for Dad. It was terrible to watch him distressed and unsettled for much of the day and his behaviour delayed, by many hours, a pelvic X-ray being done. We were offered a follow-up CT scan; however, we refused this intervention as we felt there was nothing to be gained from it. It would just result in further time delays and more stress on Dad. In accordance with his wishes (no interventions if quality of life was no longer present), we explained that we would not consent to hip surgery if there was a break anyway, so forgoing the scan felt like a 'no-brainer' as far as Mum and I were concerned. The doctor fully understood our position, in terms of both the CT scan and the surgery, and agreed a hip operation would not be in Dad's best interest at that stage of his life – we would never have accepted anaesthetic, surgical intervention and Dad waking up with a mask covering his face, a drip in his arm, unfamiliar faces around him and a hospital stay thereafter. The doctor agreed the focus should be on pain relief, physiotherapy and referral to the community nursing home liaison team upon discharge, so we began working towards that outcome.

Mum and I were relieved we had not had to justify ourselves unnecessarily, nor argue the point on behalf of Dad. Our input had been respected, and Dad's best interest was at the centre of the decision-making about his care.

Pain, being made to stay in bed all day, a foreign clinical environment and ongoing medical observations all contributed to the distress Dad felt that day. However, to their credit, the staff who treated Dad showed kindness, patience, compassion and understanding about his situation. They largely left us alone to manage Dad, recognising our faces were familiar to him and probably the ones least likely to escalate his behaviour. They interacted with Dad the best they could, while also doing their best to 'shelter' the patients around him from the words and actions he was exhibiting, which were no doubt confronting to them and their loved ones. Part of my motivation in writing the first book was to reduce fear and raise awareness about dementia. We were lucky enough to encounter several health professionals that day who displayed awareness of the issues at play and were not perturbed by them. For that, we were very grateful.

I have worked in a public emergency department before, and my husband has clocked up more than 15 years in that setting, so I am acutely aware of the workload demands on nursing and medical staff, as well as the poor behaviour of some patients (and often their family and friends). However, this was an unfamiliar environment for Mum and constituted a highly stressful day – not only due to how terribly unsettled Dad was, and the out-of-character behaviours he was exhibiting for much of the day, but also due to the length of time everything took, the hours that passed when seemingly nothing was happening, the lack of good manners on display from some patients, and the smells, sights, sounds and equipment of a busy public emergency department. Suffice to say, when Dad was finally discharged back to his nursing home after more than 12 hours, we were desperate to get out of the hospital setting. Even more so, we couldn't wait to get Dad back to his usual surroundings and resettled in a familiar environment. As he had not mobilised at all since his fall, we knew the next 48 hours would give us a good indication of where Dad was at and what to expect as his new baseline. We also knew he would need a couple of days to rest and begin his recovery, not only from the fall, but also the emotional strain he had experienced during his hospital stay.

The next few weeks

As is often the way when the elderly fall, Dad experienced a significant decline over the following weeks. On more than one occasion, I walked out of his nursing home wondering if 'this was it' and whether I would ever see him alive again. It was a confronting thought to contemplate, despite having tried my best to prepare for the moment, and I chose not to dwell on it for fear of being consumed by 'anticipatory grief'. I was finalising the publishing of my first-ever book at that time and pulling together the launch events. I was desperately hoping Dad would not pass away before the launch date (exactly one month after his fall) when my brothers, sister-in-law and nephew were arriving from interstate to be part of the celebrations. Perhaps that sounds somewhat selfish on my part, but I think my rising anxiety was due to an understandable mishmash of many things at the time – a growing sense of impending loss and fear we might not be there when Dad took his last breath, while also feeling torn and confused between the excitement I had about the launch and my sadness around Dad's deterioration. It was a challenging time emotionally.

During those weeks, we did whatever we could to keep Dad safe and assist him to regain some strength and mobility – physiotherapy was commenced, two-person assistance was introduced for whenever he used his wheelie walker, his bed was lowered, a 'crash mat' was put down on the bedroom floor, we consented to his bed being moved against the wall (which is regarded as a 'restrictive practice') and a movement sensor was set up to capture any attempts he made to get out of bed by himself. We also did whatever we could to add meaning to his life and keep him updated about family matters. Although he was no longer able to engage in conversations the way he would have in previous years, I talked to Dad about the upcoming launch and showed him the front cover of the book (which features him). He had a cute reaction, raising his eyebrows with a smirk on his face! We told him regularly that his two sons were soon arriving from interstate, and how much they were looking forward to seeing him and taking him out for coffee. We had everything crossed he was going to make it.

A few nights after the first fall, I got a call from his nursing home to say Dad had been found on the ground next to his bed, and they suspected he'd had another fall. On this occasion, given what he had endured only a few days earlier in hospital, I asked the staff not to call an ambulance. My husband and I went straight there. There was a peacefulness about him when we walked into Dad's room that night, and it washed over me in a comforting way. It was night-time, so we had the lights dimmed and his classical music was on. He would wake for a smile of recognition and a few muttered words, sleeping in between. My husband gave him a shave, the nurse on duty did regular observations (which were steady). The hours we spent there felt serene. I updated my brothers as I went to collect Mum, who was at a social event close by, and I walked out of his facility late that night not really knowing where he was at or what to expect from the next 24–48 hours. Dad seemed at peace – had he given up his fight for life and was now ready to leave us? I half-expected to be back at the nursing home in a few hours' time, sitting with Dad to accompany him into death.

Twelve days later, we had another night-time call from the nursing home, this time to report they were awaiting paramedic transfer to hospital. Staff were concerned Dad had aspirated (i.e. food, liquid, saliva or vomit had entered his airway and may end up in his lungs); his pulse was elevated, his oxygen saturation levels were concerning, and he had a phlegmy cough. Once again, my husband and I said a quick goodnight to our teenagers, jumped in the car and went straight there.

We could have refused transfer to hospital that night, given Dad's highly stressful trip to emergency just over a fortnight earlier but, when we arrived, he was already settled on the paramedics' trolley. He gave us a happy hello, so I jumped in the back of the ambulance and we crossed our fingers for a quick visit and a return home as soon as possible. I felt confident in our ability to argue against admission, if this was even suggested (which it wasn't), but in the short ride to hospital I realised antibiotics might be recommended for Dad. This revived the thought of 'no interventions to prolong life'. Where did we sit with antibiotics? Would I consent to those or not? It was a stark reminder of how even the clearest of wishes can feel 'murky' when you are in the moment and faced with making decisions about someone's care when they no longer have the capacity to do so themselves.

Fortunately, Dad was completely settled on this occasion, asleep most of the time. He didn't need any interventions and there was no requirement for treatment of any kind. The visit wasn't overly quick – we were still there long enough for bloods to be processed and regular observations to be done – but it was quick by an overcrowded emergency department's standard, and we were relieved to have Dad back to the nursing home in the early hours of the morning. Driving home that night, my husband and I agreed there would be no more trips to hospital for Dad. Enough was enough.

"I'm dying"

On one occasion, during those weeks when Mum was visiting, Dad said straight out to her, "I'm dying". Although she was taken aback by his insight, it was obviously confronting for her to hear, Mum acknowledged Dad's words and affirmed to him we knew he was tired and how hard everything was getting for him. She was very upset when she arrived home later in the day, and we had a good cry together about his awareness, his words and the inevitability of the stage Dad had reached.

As sad as it was to be facing his death head-on now, I actually took some comfort from Dad's insight into his situation, given he was obviously comfortable voicing the words 'I'm dying' to his wife of over 60 years. To me, Dad's lucidity in that moment suggested he had accepted his upcoming death and was now preparing the rest of us for it in his usual pragmatic way. There's something about that scenario, even now, that brings me peace. I'm not entirely sure what it is, but I think it's the assumption that Dad, amid the confusion of advanced dementia, had been able to take back some control over his life and where it was now headed. He had always been a list maker and somehow it felt like he was formulating his own 'timeframe to die' in a list:

1. Acceptance – tick
2. Tell others – tick
3. Have a final hoorah (still outstanding)
4. Start making my way to the other side (in progress).

That felt like the Dad of old; the Dad we had always known – organised and efficient until the end!

Two final celebrations

Two weeks after the fall we thought may have broken Dad's hip, Father's Day rolled around and then, a week later, his 87th birthday arrived – we happily ticked off two milestones we had only dared hope we might reach. There were no raucous parties or wild dances for either occasion, though there were smiles, small wins and plenty of reasons to feel grateful:

- He was up and about with his walker, had a nice meal (including a beer) and played a ball-throwing game with my husband at the nursing home's early Father's Day celebrations.

- Although he was quite drowsy and in a wheelchair, we were able to take Dad off the facility's grounds on Father's Day so he could enjoy some sun and, most importantly, some ice-cream.
- On the day of his birthday, he was able to venture outside with his walker so we could sit around the table sharing cake together.

On the night of Dad's birthday – 11 September, just over three weeks after his first fall – I reflected on the fact I had celebrated both occasions for the final time with Dad, at least in person. I knew he would not be with us in twelve months' time and, in my head, I suspected he probably wouldn't make it to Christmas either, given it was still three months away. It was confronting, and my heart hurt. However, I re-read the 'Gratitude' chapter in my previous book and put up the following post on Facebook:

> There's a chapter in the book about gratitude, which closes with this statement – '*There are opportunities for gratefulness all around us. Sometimes we just have to open our eyes (and our hearts) to find them.*' Dad was the inspiration for this book. I'm so grateful we got to see him today, on his 87th birthday.

That post pretty much sums up how I felt that night, knowing we were observing a rapid decline in Dad's physical health, but being so thankful for the long life he'd had and the many wonderful family memories we would always treasure.

The final hoorah

A few days after his birthday, the 'tough old bird' (as my brother was calling Dad by that stage) got a second wind and he was in fabulous form for our interstate visitors! For Dad, nothing was more important than his family. He had thrown his energy into many other pursuits over the years and focussed his priorities wherever they had needed to be; he farmed for decades, flew a small plane and achieved a number of things as an active community member. But, above all, he was proud of every one of his family members and he loved having them around him. That week, there was my book launch, as well as walks, wheelchair taxi rides, trips out for lunch or coffee, visits to his nursing home and 'pushes' along the waterfront. We even managed a trip to the post office to take passport photos for a taxi subsidy application form! They were precious days for all of us, and I'm so grateful for them.

It is my firm belief that:

- Dad felt a sense of peace and closure at the end of that week, having been surrounded by his beloved family.

- His soul was happy.

- He was comfortable, at that point, to start the process of 'letting go' and actively moving towards the end of his life.

And that's exactly what he did.

THREE

Getting our 'ducks in a row'

So, what did all this mean in terms of care provision, expected time-frames and preparing for death?

People in the advanced stage of dementia often exhibit symptoms suggesting that they are getting closer to death, but they may, in fact, live with these symptoms for many months. This uncertainty makes it difficult to plan for the end of their life. This is complicated by the fact that, due to their cognitive decline, they are unable to articulate what they need to be more comfortable as the end of their life approaches. Having observed Dad's deterioration and accepted we were 'on the downhill slide', as his enduring power of attorney it suddenly became very important for me to acquire knowledge and prepare myself for what to expect going forward. This would make me feel empowered, and make me an effective support for Mum, but it's also what would ensure I was making decisions that would be in Dad's best interest when the time came.

The pacemaker issue

Dad had already been diagnosed with dementia when his pacemaker was implanted. As he was in the much earlier stages of the disease in those days, we would never have considered refusing that medical recommendation at the time. However, after his first fall and the significant deterioration we were witnessing, the issue of Dad's pacemaker began to trouble me. I'd had questions about the reality for end of life when you have a pacemaker in the back of my mind for some time, and the 'noise' surrounding this issue was getting louder and louder:

- A 'normal' heart stops beating when the rest of the body stops working and shuts down; would Dad's pacemaker automatically cease working?

- Could we request it be 'deactivated', given Dad was in steady decline and had indicated years before he didn't want interventions keeping him alive in the absence of quality of life?

- If so, would this require surgical intervention? And when/where/how would we do that?

I knew there were different types of pacemakers and I needed to understand what we were dealing with in Dad's case. I sought advice from several different sources, and it was a frustrating 'investigation':

- A doctor told me she had enquired in the past about 'turning off' a patient's pacemaker (when her patient stated she had no quality of life and wanted to die) and been told she risked being charged with manslaughter if she did so.

- Others in the health profession told me that to suggest someone could be charged with manslaughter was a 'ridiculous turn of phrase', and indicated that a pacemaker could be deactivated, with magnets, if that was in the best interest of a dying person.

- Someone else suggested the battery running out would be the only course of action available to us, and this would likely not be for a few more years.

- An aged care employee advised me to prepare for the eventuality she had witnessed, on more than one occasion, when a pacemaker continued to facilitate a heartbeat long after it was obvious her client had stopped breathing.

Oh my goodness, I was getting more and more confused (as well as more and more frustrated) about what we might expect, and it was causing me consternation. I was already witnessing a steady decline in my dad's health and a quick march towards the end of his life. I just wanted a definitive answer so that I knew where we stood, what to expect and how best to prepare.

After going around in bureaucratic circles, I finally tracked down the surgeon who had implanted Dad's device five years earlier. They told me, categorically, that his device would stop as soon as he took his last breath. As much as I desperately wanted to trust their information, if I'm honest, I never completely relaxed about the possibility of Dad's heart continuing to beat until such time as he **did** take his last breath and immediately had no further pulse. What a ride that issue turned out to be. It's crazy how overwhelming these scenarios feel when you are staring the death of a loved one in the face and you are desperate for certainty and reassurance however, and wherever, you can get it. Of course, the hard truth is that we can't control everything, no matter how hard we try. But, for me, I had to know I had researched this issue to the best of my ability in order to quieten the noise in my head and prepare us for what to expect from Dad's death.

A month before death

Knowing he was on the 'downhill slide', at the end of October I requested a meeting with the nursing home's care manager to get her opinion on Dad's life expectancy. His disease progression had hastened, and he had become significantly frailer since his fall in August, with a particularly rapid decline during the last four weeks. There were late-stage dementia symptoms that indicated we were now moving from a passive palliative pathway to an active end-of-life pathway. We were most likely inside the last months, or perhaps even weeks, of Dad's life. As you have read already, by that time I felt it was unlikely he would be with us for Christmas, and I felt confident we would be able to grant Dad the wish he had always made clear to us – a wish not to 'linger' for a long time.

The clinical indicators we discussed were that:

- Dad's fatigue and lethargy had increased, and he was becoming less and less interested in going out of the nursing home (something he had always wanted to do previously) or joining in with activities.

- He was very tired most of the time, sleeping a lot more and not always able to be woken when we visited.

- His muscle tone was decreasing, hence the falling and difficulty with weightbearing.

- His mobility was impacted – walking was becoming harder, slower and less appealing, and he required at least a wheelie walker or, more often than not, a wheelchair.

- His speech was becoming very quiet, often just a whisper and only a few words at a time.

- He was fully dependent on personal care staff for toileting, showering and dressing.

- He had a reduced desire to eat and take in fluids and had been experiencing ongoing weight loss over a period of time. There was agreement to cease his supplements, as they had not stabilised his weight loss and were, at times, more of a hassle than anything else.

While the care manager was obviously unable to provide an exact timeframe, we agreed it would be no surprise if Dad died within the next couple of months. All the indications suggested that he had reached the terminal phase of his disease, and we could now withdraw medications that would serve no further therapeutic purpose and focus on optimising his comfort.

Permission to die

Around this time, I suggested to Mum we should start giving Dad 'permission' to die. This was not only letting him know we understood he was tired and acknowledging how hard everything was getting for him but, perhaps even more importantly, reassuring him we were comfortable with him starting to let go of life when he was ready to do so. In addition to my own personal (and professional) experiences of people 'hanging on to life' for a specific event, I had heard many stories of those dying waiting for particular people to arrive, perhaps partly because they were seeking their permission to die.

This proposition was too confronting for Mum. She wasn't ready to start having direct conversations like that with Dad just yet. Given he had been 'providing' for Mum all their married life, I was very sure (dementia or not) he needed to hear those words from Mum first. This would then mean he'd know he was no longer obligated to care for her and that she would be able to manage, with the full support of her family, without him. I was confident Mum would soon reach a stage where she could have these conversations. Indeed, not long after, Mum returned home from visiting Dad one day and told me she had reached that point and said several things to him for the first time. Despite how confronting this idea had been for her initially, she did feel relief at saying the things she did and was glad she had verbalised to him that he could start letting go of life whenever he was ready. Knowing Mum had taken this step, I prioritised saying similar things to Dad from the next time I saw him, and continued to do so until he took his last breath. I truly believe passing on these words is an act of selflessness that anyone supporting a dying person should consider – yes, it's confronting to say out loud to someone you love that you are happy for them to die, but it's also a way to ease the suffering and guilt they might feel about leaving their loved ones.

Simple pleasures

Knowing he was getting closer to death, there were a few simple things we really wanted to do while Dad was still able to leave his nursing home. However, as a hoist had been required to get him up on a couple of occasions, we didn't want to make things traumatic for him in any way. We did have to reschedule our plans a couple of times when it wouldn't have been in Dad's best interest to force him getting out of bed, but thankfully we managed to achieve everything we had hoped for, even in spite of some lingering COVID-19 restrictions at the aged care facility. Those things were:

- Taking some final photos of Dad with our teenage children.

- Getting him out in the wheelchair taxi for a final ride to a spot by the water we had taken him many times before, including as recently as a few weeks earlier when we had shared a family lunch. This is a local spot we still visit, which will always hold a special place in our hearts. Little more than a month after Dad died, I had a photo shoot at this location to accompany an article written about my first book, which was published as a legacy for Dad. As you can imagine, these photos made that story very special for me, and I enjoy looking back at them.

- Getting him out in the sunshine for a ride in the wheelchair whenever he could – even if it was only around the block. These simple little walks, where he sometimes patted a dog or two, pointed out flowers or got a smile from someone, were precious moments. We walked away feeling so grateful for the time we'd had (unlike the shock and trauma of an unplanned death, where no one has time to enjoy the final life pleasures with someone). Each of these walks, even if they were only 25 minutes, felt special by the virtue that it may be the last walk we ever had together.

On one of these walks around the block with Dad in his wheelchair, I took a selfie of him and me and showed him the photo. He smiled, pointed at me and said, "Lisa". It very nearly brought me undone – I will never forget it. It was such a clear indicator to me that (as my brother described it) 'old memories run deep', and it felt so wonderful hearing Dad identify me in that photo. It affirmed for me that, even at that late stage in his illness, he felt safe with me and enjoyed being with me. There had been times earlier in Dad's nursing home stay when he had been unable to introduce me by name or, on one occasion, explain the relationship between him and me to one of the facility's carers. This never bothered me at all, because I always knew who he was! His connection to me, and his calmness around me, was always enough to suggest I was someone Dad felt safe and comfortable with and, really, that's all I ever cared about.

So, we knew where we were at, where we were headed and what to expect. It sounds like we were completely settled, right? Well, as it turns out, we weren't …

FOUR

A lot can happen in 12 days

A total change of plan

Having specifically sought out the care manager's input about an expected timeframe, and agreeing it would be no surprise if Dad's life was to come to an end within the next couple of months, feelings of discomfort and anxiety began growing in me over the next fortnight. I was finding it harder and harder to say goodbye to Dad after visiting, and both Mum and I were barely able to do this without tears. The decline in his physical health had been rapid, the frailty was so obvious, and the enormity of 'the task of living' was looking so very overwhelming for Dad. I found myself worrying more and more that he may end up dying without a family presence. I somehow got it into my head that he was going to die in the middle of the night, so I was now measuring all my (largely irrational) thoughts against that assumption:

- What if his slide into death happened so quickly we couldn't make it?

- What if we didn't hear the phone when the nursing home called us?

- What if only one of us was there to accompany him into death? How would that feel for the others?

- Imagine how lonely it would feel to transition into death by yourself, with no family or even staff with you?

The height of the COVID-19 pandemic was not far behind us, and I think we all felt deeply for those who died during those dark times, sometimes alone and very often without their loved ones around them. I was becoming almost paranoid about my mobile phone, constantly checking and rechecking the volume was at the highest level and that I hadn't accidentally turned on flight mode or missed any calls. I had the phone right next to my bed and, unsurprisingly, was sleeping poorly every night. Although we had issued these instructions verbally, I emailed the care manager, reiterating we wanted to be contacted, regardless of the time of day or night, to ensure we were able to get to Dad as soon as possible if it looked like he was rapidly deteriorating. In among all this, I was working part-time, running a household, transporting the kids to various activities and trying to keep myself fit, healthy and sane! I was on an emotional rollercoaster and really didn't know what was happening to me and why, all of a sudden, the idea of Dad's death was becoming so unsettling and hard for me to manage:

- Was I in denial he was dying?
- Hadn't I prepared myself for this inevitability for many months already?
- Shouldn't he be allowed to seek out peace for himself, as soon as possible, if that's where he was at?

Part of our criteria when looking for a nursing home had been that they offered end-of-life care, yet here I was leaving him one Sunday evening, after helping him with his dinner, berating myself for having ever put him into a nursing home in the first place. I was bawling, sitting in the carpark outside his facility and consumed by guilt that it had been me who had effectively 'called time' on Dad living at home with us two years earlier due to the stress and ongoing emotional impact on Mum. Why hadn't I just somehow made it work and kept him home with us so we wouldn't be in this position? Why? Why? Why?

Through the guilt and self-blame I had never before felt about Dad going into care, somehow a random thought that 'maybe we could bring him home' forced its way into my head … yes, he had deteriorated a lot and we would probably need some help … but maybe, just maybe, it wasn't too late to facilitate him dying at home … then we could be there with him around the clock … could we really do that? … would we be allowed? … would it be in his best interest? … how would we do that? …

Oh man, there was a lot running through my head. Why was all this happening, and what was going on? I was so confused by my own feelings, and where they were coming from, that I didn't even voice the possibility of moving Dad to my husband when I got home that night. I was struggling to make sense of it myself:

- Was all this about fear and I just needed to be courageous?

- Was it denial and I just needed to reach acceptance?

- Was it a lack of trust in the nursing home?

I couldn't shake the feeling, so the next morning I posed the question of transferring Dad back home to my husband. I half expected him to tell me it was far too late, given Dad's increased frailty and declining health, and that I would need to accept he was going to die in the nursing home. Instead, he immediately affirmed it was a beautiful idea and said we should try to make it work! Yes! A seed of hope had been planted inside my head, and I had something positive to cling to – thank goodness for that. I was leaving for work soon after that conversation, so I waited until later in the day when I had time to discuss my idea with Mum in more depth.

Understandably, Mum was surprised at my suggestion, not because she wasn't keen, but because it had come completely out of left field. Taking Dad out of care was something we had never discussed before – since he entered the nursing home just over two years earlier, we assumed that his life would come to an end either there or in hospital due to respiratory illness. Aside from whether or not we would be 'allowed' to bring Dad home, Mum's only real question was around the legalities of him dying at home. I knew we didn't have to be concerned about this – he had a terminal disease and there were clear clinical indicators (as explained in the previous chapter) he was very much in the terminal phase of his illness. Dad's death, however long it took, would be a natural and expected outcome, with supplementary in-home nursing and medical services engaged as required.

Once Mum, my husband and I had talked things through a little more and began formulating a plan, I set about getting the advice I needed as to **how** we would do what we wanted to do. Now I was no longer acting purely in the role of a 'daughter'; I could put my social worker hat on, make a list of tasks (thanks for those genes, Dad!) and focus on the entirety of the situation:

- What would we need on a practical level?
- Where would we get it?
- Who would do what?
- What would Dad need from us on an emotional level?

My first phone call was to Kerri-Anne. I had met her a few years earlier when I began seeking out opportunities to get involved in the dementia space, and she had become my favourite 'go-to' person for advice and information about all things dementia. Having founded a local in-home nursing and home hospice agency, I knew she was a wealth of knowledge in the palliative care sector and would be able to explain exactly what options we had and what we would need. Kerri-Anne immediately gave me the injection of confidence I needed! Although she indicated it wasn't common to take someone out of a nursing home and bring them home to die, she also said 'anything is possible' and that it would be 'the best gift' we could give Dad. With those comments under my belt, I never once questioned whether we were doing the right thing by Dad as we moved forward. I had no fear about him dying in my presence – in fact, that would be my best-case scenario. I knew Mum was also hoping to be present when Dad took his last breath, so I tapped into an inner sense of confidence and took on the attitude that I was going to make it happen. Now it was a matter of getting everything we needed together as quickly as possible so we were ready to go when we felt the time was right.

The (practical) things we needed to provide best-practice end-of-life care, and where we would get them

- A hospital bed, both for Dad's comfort and functionality for us as his carers – these beds are fully adjustable, meaning different sections of the bed can be raised or lowered to alleviate pressure and improve circulation. Kerri-Anne knew of one that had been donated, but it is something we would have hired from a local healthcare supplies outlet if that had not been the case.

- A pressure-relieving (inflatable) air mattress – these mattresses provide support for the head and body and relieve stress on pressure points. This was something we were able to easily hire from the local healthcare supplies outlet.

- A slide sheet – this is basically a 'slippery' sheet that makes it quicker, easier, safer and more comfortable to reposition people. This was something we purchased from the local healthcare supplies outlet.

- Support – it was important to us that Mum didn't feel burdened by a 'carer' role and would not end up burnt out by the experience. We wanted her to get a decent sleep each night and just focus on being Dad's wife and chief companion for however long he had left. Initially, we weren't sure whether we would need supplementary in-home support or not, and this was something we felt happy to 'play by ear'. My

husband and I were comfortable providing personal care ourselves and knew we could always access additional nursing
services (privately), depending on how long Dad lived for
and if we needed a break. Several friends also offered to sit
with Dad, so we knew we could source additional help if we
needed it.

- Medications – what did we want available for effective relief
of symptoms and pain? We assumed Dad's GP would be
happy to write scripts for what we required, and that we
would fill these ourselves at a local pharmacy. If this was not
the case, we knew we had the backup option of accessing
scripts via the palliative care nurse practitioner on Kerri-
Anne's team.

- A healthy stash of continence aids, washcloths, towels,
sheets, pillows and cushions to keep Dad clean and optimise
his comfort.

The (non-practical) things Dad was going to need from us

- We knew we had to get comfortable with the uncertainty
around how long Dad might live for once we got him home,
so I set about creating a 'contingency plan' across all other
areas of our lives (work, kids' activities, volunteer roles)
for the upcoming weeks. My husband's long service leave
was approved, from whenever he wanted to take it and for
however long he needed, and I advised my clients I was
likely to be unavailable for a period of time once we had Dad
home. For us, it came down to priorities – caring for Dad at
home was going to be our number one priority once the time
came, and everything (and everyone) else would either have
to fit around that task or drop off the calendar.

- It goes without saying that, on an emotional level, Dad was
going to need kindness and compassion, clear explanations

of anything we were doing in terms of personal care or medication, the comfort of familiar faces, normality around him, a nice place to die (with a view he could enjoy) and a constant eye on his needs as he moved closer to death. My husband had lovingly tended to various ailments and injuries of Dad's over the years, and Dad had always been extremely comfortable receiving care from him. So, him taking on the lead care role was never going to be an issue. As his 'assistant', I knew it would be important for me to appear confident, calm and relaxed around Dad so there was, to him, no mistaking:

- We were choosing to bring him home and care for him out of love for him.

- We were comfortable with, and not scared of, the dying process.

- We were ready to let him go, meaning any sadness he observed from us was very normal.

Updating the family

The one thing I always knew as we travelled the dementia path with Dad over several years was that Mum and I had the unwavering support of both my brothers in any of the care decisions we made. Technology certainly has its downsides but, given our family is spread across three Australian states, I'm grateful we live in the era of video calling, voice messaging, texting and email. Not only could I easily keep my brothers regularly updated, but both of them could stay in constant contact with Mum and also see Dad via video. This was important when he could no longer carry on an independent conversation with them anymore – at least they were able to remain connected to him by being able to see him.

My brothers always took the view that, as Mum and I were 'on the ground' and knew what was happening on a daily basis, we were best placed to assess a situation, deal with whatever it threw at us and make ongoing decisions. I always valued their input and asked their advice at times, knowing they were unlikely to argue against anything Mum and I felt was in Dad's best interest, nor stand in the way of us making decisions we believed were right. Deciding to bring Dad home to die was undeniably the biggest decision Mum, my husband and I had made since we had put Dad into care two years earlier. Given the idea had come out of left field, I knew it would come as a shock to my brothers to hear, so I waited until I knew exactly what we would need and had a pretty good idea how we would manage the situation before I contacted them both. While they were surprised to hear about the change, they were immediately supportive of the revised plan, and we began discussing when the best time to return for a visit would be. Given they were juggling work commitments, and we were unsure exactly when Dad would come home, or how long he would live once he did, these were daily conversations with ongoing updates right through until the day Dad died.

Liaison with the nursing home

It was time to speak to the care manager again, this time to advise her we had decided to move Dad back home. Only a fortnight had passed since I had last sat down with her to get her best estimate of a timeframe for Dad's death. Although she confirmed that removing a resident and taking them home to die was not a common process, she also said there was no reason it couldn't be done and that it would be a lovely thing to do for Dad. She later told me she had never had a family remove their loved one from an aged care facility and take them home to die. That conversation helped me realise there was a need to share our story and educate families about end-of-life choices.

As we discussed the finer details, we agreed that getting the timing right – not too early but also not in the active dying phase – would be key if the experience was going to be in Dad's best interest. She confirmed he would need to be bedfast (no longer mobile) and no longer taking in food and drink to a life-sustainable level, and felt that would be soon but was not necessarily imminent. That night, I dealt with the paperwork to facilitate Dad's discharge when the time came and ticked off another step in the process.

Telling Dad about the change of plan

So, when did Dad find out about the change of plan and that he would, in fact, be granted the opportunity to die at home? One of my nephews had been visiting from interstate over the weekend and it was a Monday afternoon – exactly one week after I had first floated the idea with Mum, and five days after I had spoken to the care manager about our change of plan. Once again, I went to the nursing home and, with her, I went through the 'indicators' we had previously agreed would show us we were ready to transfer Dad home – he was now eating and drinking very little and was bedfast (he had not been out of bed for the preceding four days). The time was right, and he was ready to go. The care manager committed to speaking with Dad's treating doctor the following day so the wheels could be set in motion.

I left her office and went straight around to see Dad. I knew it would be an emotional occasion and I could feel a sense of anticipation rising in me the closer I got to his room. I will hold the memories of my conversation with Dad that afternoon very close to my heart for the rest of my life. His classical music was on, and he was lying quietly in bed, looking up at the ceiling and around the tops of the walls, like he often did. We were never sure, but it often appeared as though he was seeing things or perhaps even people from his past we couldn't see. By this stage, perhaps it was a pre-death vision? We'll never know, and it doesn't really matter – he was at peace. I sat down on the side of Dad's bed, took his hand and announced myself. As was always the way, I got a smile, which suggested he either knew who I was or, at the very least, recognised me as someone he knew well and felt safe and comfortable with. Almost immediately I began to cry, and so did he. There was suddenly this incredible connection between Dad and I as he locked eyes with me and held my gaze, without interruption, for the entire 20 minutes:

- I told him we would be taking him home soon and we were going to look after him.
- I told him we were looking forward to having him back home in the next few days and that we had a bed ready for him.
- I told him this was something we **wanted** to do, in the hope he wouldn't feel like a burden or as if we felt forced to do this.
- I reiterated he had our 'permission' to die whenever he'd had enough, and that Mum would be well looked after by our family.
- Speaking for both me and my brothers, I reminded him how much we all loved him and how many cherished memories we had to draw on.
- I explained how much we would miss him, but how we would have each other for comfort when those feelings became overwhelming.

To be honest, I was pretty much a stuck record! I just kept saying the same things repeatedly, partly because I needed to leave no doubt in Dad's mind about anything I was saying to him, and partly because I could barely stand to walk away from such a precious moment and break the connection between us – Dad had tears running down his face for the whole time, and so did I, but he was smiling. Smiling! I knew he understood, and I knew he was happy with the news I had brought that day. It was a very powerful experience.

You may have heard the phrase 'terminal lucidity', which refers to an end-of-life energy surge often seen in the hours or days leading up to a person's death. It may see a dying person demonstrate clarity in their thinking, or when saying words, that had been absent until that point. Is that what was going on that day? I don't know, but there is absolutely no doubt in my mind Dad knew exactly what I was explaining to him – he contributed to the verbal exchange in his own limited way, quietly whispering words I couldn't make out, and holding on to my hands as hard as he could. I have recounted this story on several occasions since that day and it still makes me emotional every time, including now as I write these words. It was an unexpected, and welcome, display of complete clarity. And, if I'd had any doubt about our decision to transfer Dad home to die (which I hadn't), it would have been erased by that conversation. I felt totally affirmed with our plan of action.

When I left Dad's room that afternoon, I also left behind the feelings of rising anxiety and panic I had been carrying around for the last few weeks. I had now told him of our intention to take him home and how we were going to care for him. Knowing I had said all those things, and that he had fully understood every word, meant I was no longer worried or uptight about the possibility of him dying without me present. I specifically remember thinking: *if Dad dies in the next couple of days, before we have had a chance to get him home, I will be okay with that*. The intention had been set, he knew what that intention was (to get him home as soon as possible), and it was now his choice if he wanted to spare us the experience of being with him as he took his last breath. I also recall how I felt a certain sense of 'confidence in the universe' to deliver what we were planning for – I was very sure it was what Dad wanted and that he knew he did not have to spare us being there at the end.

Prepared and ready to go

While I was visiting Dad the next day, I took a call from his treating GP, who had been looking after him in the nursing home for several months. Having only heard about our intention to take Dad home earlier that day, she understandably had questions about our plans for caring for him. However, once she ascertained he would be safe with us upon discharge, and that we were well prepared and had the capacity and necessary resources to provide high-quality end-of-life care for Dad, she offered us her full support:

- She explained that public ambulance transfer from the facility to home would need to be facilitated by her and that she would organise this as soon as possible. We had investigated doing this privately ourselves, but the wait time for service would have been similar and the cost prohibitive for what is barely a two-kilometre journey!
- She confirmed she would provide scripts for all medications we may require for Dad at the end of his life, including those for managing secretions and pain.
- She offered to visit us at home if we needed her medical support and/or advice at any point and said she would complete the death certificate when the time came.

The following day, my husband and I went to visit Dad and found him quite animated, laughing and pointing at things; a significantly different presentation to how he had been over the previous week. We knew it's common in people nearing the end of their life to have an 'uptick' like this in their energy levels, and we walked out of there laughing about exactly how long we may end up nursing Dad at home for! However, as you'll read in the next chapter, when he vacated his room at the nursing home the next day, he was back to sleeping a lot and was well on his way to dying.

The feelings that led to a total change of plan

It took comments from other people to help me make sense of what was going on with my feelings and emotions over those few weeks. It was only after I spoke to others about the upset and discomfort that had crept into my head, and my uncertainty as to why that had happened, that I reached my conclusion – Dad himself was responsible for planting the seeds of confusion in my head. I will always be so glad he did!

Family was the most important thing in Dad's life, and I'm certain he wanted at least some of us to be there for the end so he was not alone, not feeling powerless and not without control over his own circumstances. I truly believe he knew he was nearing the end of his life, that he was ready to go and that he wanted to get back home to leave us in the most peaceful, dignified way. Furthermore, I truly believe he was 'channelling' his energy (around the emotions of dying) for me to absorb, perhaps knowing that him dying at home would be a 'gift' for us, as well as for him. I've always had a strong connection with Dad, and I am sure he would have known he could 'reach' me if he persisted and that I would be able to 'make it happen' for him. I'm equally sure he would not have wanted to put this confusion onto Mum, or burden her with the responsibility of picking up his energy and acting on it. In summary, and call me kooky or even weird, I am thoroughly convinced that Dad:

- was ready to die

- wanted to do so in a peaceful, dignified manner

- wanted the comfort, security and familiarity of his home environment

- wanted at least some of his family around him

- had confidence in my ability to make it happen for him

- channelled his energy to me, creating confusion and upset in the process, but ultimately allowing me to grab hold of the seed he planted in my head and make it grow into a reality for him.

Whatever it was that forced me to look outside the expected scenario and completely change it, I will be forever grateful for how the whole process panned out. At the end of the day, it's almost irrelevant how, or even why, we changed the plan. The most important thing is that we realised we had a choice and chose to exercise it to create a good death for Dad. Detailing our story and explaining our choice was a large part of my motivation for writing this book. I really want people to know there are choices around death and that plans can always be changed.

FIVE

Coming home

Twelve days after I sat in the carpark of his residential aged care facility, bawling my eyes out and berating myself for having put him into care, Dad was on his way home. The nursing home had done a good job of caring for him. They had always been open to feedback, questions and suggestions and, most importantly, Dad had been happy there since the day he moved in. Despite this, I knew we could deliver a better standard of care for him because we were his family and loved him more than anyone else could be expected to. He left the premises with a guard of honour up the hallway, something I have since learnt is always the practice when someone leaves their facility after passing away. Dad was sleeping peacefully as the paramedics wheeled him out; nevertheless, we felt this was a beautiful touch and a true mark of respect for the time he had spent in their care.

Meant to be

There are two 'funny' little memories from the day Dad arrived home that, for us at least, can only be described as serendipitous. They are of no clinical significance, but they are details that affirmed for me that bringing Dad home was 'meant to be':

- It was 23 November 2023 (23/11/23) – earlier that morning I had been talking to my eldest brother interstate, who

suggested it would be fitting for Dad to arrive home
at 11:23am that day. We had a joke about that, from a
numerological point of view, and left it in the hands of the
ambulance transport service – after all, this was the one
thing we could not control, given it was totally dependent
on their competing priorities and workload. As the morning
passed and the clock ticked past 11:23am, I updated him on
the fact we had missed our window of time. We laughed it
off and we left it at that. Two hours later, at exactly 1:23pm,
the paramedics wheeled Dad in the front door and he
was home. Incredibly, due to the time difference between
Australian states, this was 11:23am in our (spiritual) home
state of Western Australia – where I grew up and where Dad
spent more than 50 years of his life! Coincidence? Chance?
Fluke? Luck? Unrelated? Who knows, but for us it felt like
an auspicious start to a good death, and it put a smile on all
our faces.

- As Dad was wheeled inside, one of the paramedics noticed a
photo on the wall in Mum's flat that piqued his interest. He
asked a question about it, and so unfolded a conversation that
confirmed he knew a few of the same people we knew from
Western Australia, including some he had very recently been
in touch with! Once again, you can ignore this exchange and
afford it no time or significance but, for us, it was comforting and reassuring to know this lovely man and his shift
partner had delivered our 'precious cargo' (as he had referred
to Dad when he opened up the back of the ambulance at the
top of our driveway) home for the final time. Out of all the
paramedics who were rostered on for work that day, we had a
'three degrees of separation' connection with him that criss-
crossed Australia, a geographical distance of approximately
4,500 kilometres!

Settling in

Dad was immediately settled, unconfused about his transition and aware of the fact he had come home. Although my husband has an extensive nursing background and has cared for the sick and dying in a critical hospital setting many times over, he is not an expert in palliative dementia care, and it was important for Mum and me to ask our own questions of someone who is. This was my friend Kerri-Anne, who arrived that afternoon. Her nursing agency would be supporting us, as required, and we needed to understand for ourselves:

- What to expect (clinically) over the coming days as Dad progressed towards death.

- What support we might need from her agency, how much would be available to us and how much it would cost.

- What paperwork would be required at the time of Dad's death and who could complete it.

- How long after he died would we be permitted to have Dad at home?

- How would medications be administered?

Having assessed Dad, she answered all our questions and invited us to contact her when we needed support over the following days. As his GP had agreed to provide scripts for any medications we might require, we didn't need assistance from her agency in that regard; however, she went through the dosing and drug administration regimen with us so we would be prepared in advance.

One of the most pressing things on my mind was how I would satisfy myself we were not starving or dehydrating Dad, given he had reached a stage of eating very little and had clearly lost almost all his desire to take in food and liquids. When he was a resident in the nursing home, this had been their domain – although Mum and I had assisted him with meals for some time by then, we weren't the ones bringing his meals, or making decisions about what to offer him and when. But now he was home, that was suddenly in our hands.

Obviously, we didn't want to cause Dad to aspirate, but starvation was not a nice thought either. In straightforward language we could easily understand, Kerri-Anne explained that Dad's body was already in the process of shutting down and that he likely had very little, if any, appetite. She gave the very simple advice of 'offer, but don't force', indicating Dad would let us know whether he was interested in taking in any food or drink we might offer. Put simply, he was going to die from his terminal illness, not because of starvation. Kerri-Anne gave us some foam mouth swab sticks for oral care and hydration, and we bought some yoghurt, some Sustagen, some lemonade and a 'sippy cup' with a straw, unsure if we would use any of those things but preferring to have them all on hand should we need them. We had the scripts filled, and I felt ready for the task ahead. Dad was home, he was in safe hands, and it was time to give him a dignified death.

What happened to the dementia?

I remember commenting to my husband after Dad had been home for a day or so that there was no obvious indication of dementia anymore – he was calm, peaceful and sleepy, just like any other elderly man at the end of his life:

- He was immobile, so there was no shadowing people, wandering off, moving everything around or getting up during the night multiple times, which there had been previously when he lived at home with dementia.

- He was speaking very little, so the words he was saying were less muddled and there wasn't the repetition of questions and instructions, nor the emphatic rejection of rational explanations for things he couldn't accept, as there had been in the past.

- He was no longer changing his clothes many times in a day, putting his shoes off and on, or struggling with his buttons.

- There was no restlessness or picking up and putting down tasks and activities repeatedly, as there had been previously.

This realisation was quite moving and very much affirmed for me that our decision to bring Dad home had been the right one. Putting him into care two years earlier had taken a big dose of courage and been a momentous family decision. It came from needing to protect Mum and allow her to let go of her overwhelming 24/7 caring role before she 'collapsed' herself, both physically and mentally. Given that all the challenging changed behaviours were now absent, we were back to being able to care for Dad in the best way we could. Even better, Mum was able to capitalise on the time she had left with her husband of over 60 years as the dying man he was, not as a man who required around-the-clock supervision and a high level of care from her.

What did (high-quality) end-of-life care at home actually look like?

As we went along, I learnt quickly from my husband what it takes to be a compassionate nursing aide! I also immediately realised something I hadn't yet had the headspace to really reflect on – the great honour one feels at being able to care for someone at the end of their life (particularly if that someone has cared for and about you over the course of your lifetime). In hindsight, I think there probably is no greater honour. I am beyond grateful my husband and I had the opportunity to do this for Dad together, with Mum alongside us.

For the six days he was at home with us, Dad's hospital bed took centre stage in the flat's living room. Mum sat with Dad a lot, my husband slept on a mattress next to him overnight, and we came in and out constantly throughout the day – the kids did the same – and life went on around Dad, albeit a little quieter than in former, rowdier days! The focus was on companionship, reassurance, comfort care and being proactive about symptom management. In terms of the practicalities:

- We positioned the bed so Dad was looking out the window, with a view of trees, grass and flowers (in fact, the cover of the book is inspired by the view Dad had during his days at home). We kept chairs next to him so we could hold his hand whenever we wanted to, and so we could show him things and he could easily hear us whenever we spoke to him.

- We changed Dad's position regularly to prevent pressure sores and moisturised the areas of his body prone to developing hard patches. This was always preceded by a simple explanation for Dad as to who was there, what we were doing, how we were going to do it and how long it would take.

- We had classical music running in the background. This has always been Dad's preferred genre; one of the only genres he truly liked.

- In addition to what was required for ongoing bowel care and incontinence, we gave Dad a bed bath and change of shirt each morning to freshen him up, and a facial shave every couple of days.

- We made sure to keep Dad's mouth clean and moist and his lips hydrated. This was not only to maximise his comfort but also to ensure he would be able to communicate with us if he was trying to. These tasks made Mum, my husband and me feel close to Dad; a way of actively supporting him to prepare for a peaceful, dignified death.

- We kept an ongoing check on Dad's physical surroundings to ensure the room was at a comfortable temperature and he was not at risk of getting cold, overheating or feeling stuffy.

- Perhaps most importantly, we took a vigilant approach to pain management and symptom control, not only to avoid any terminal agitation (anxious, restless behaviour that can occur in the days before death), but also to ensure tasks like turning and bathing remained pain-free. Given Dad was not able to verbally communicate discomfort as some others can, even at the very end of their lives, it was important to look for grimaces or other physical reactions that may have been responses to pain and then act accordingly.

On his fifth day at home, we had a second visit from Kerri-Anne, who was satisfied Dad was peaceful and that his pain relief seemed suitable. Up until the afternoon before, he had not required any injections for symptom control; however, as the intervals between injections had begun to shorten by the time of her visit, we decided to introduce a subcutaneous 'butterfly cannula' (a small plastic tube inserted into the tissue so medication can be given again and again into the same site). We had the option of utilising a syringe driver (a small, portable, battery-operated device that administers continuous medication subcutaneously over a selected time period); however, Dad appeared comfortable with 'dosing on demand' so we didn't feel we needed to take that step at that point. Given the lack of food and drink Dad had taken in over the previous three days, Kerri-Anne predicted we were well inside the last 72 hours of Dad's life and suggested she check in again the next day. As it turns out, we did see her the next day, this time to 'verify' Dad's death and complete the Life Extinct Form (as it is known in Queensland) for him.

The day of Dad's death

Earlier in the morning, I had been in contact with my brothers about their arrival and, at that stage, they were gearing up to be with us in two days' time. There had been daily discussions about where Dad was at, how much longer he might live for, when they should come, how quickly they could get here, how much time they would have and so on. Having been with us only two months earlier, they had both left after that visit wondering if they would see Dad alive again, and were reconciled with the fact that, if they didn't, their last days with him had been fantastic, and he knew they loved him.

My husband and I did the usual midmorning bed, bath and clean shirt routine. By the time we had finished, there was an obvious change in Dad's breathing pattern. My husband suggested we ask the kids to come downstairs and sit with him for a while, potentially to say their goodbyes, and thankfully Mum had just returned from the supermarket as this significant change became apparent. From there, it was a very quick and calm process. An hour later, with light rain falling outside and us all gathered around him, Dad took his final breath.

It is widely believed that hearing is the last sense to go at death – in other words, right up until the end, a dying person will be taking comfort from their hands being held by those around them, and even more so from the familiar voices and reassuring words they are hearing. I'm certain there was no doubt in Dad's mind that he was well loved, and that our lives with him would always be fondly remembered by us. In the process of him dying, we all received a 'gift' that day – Dad experienced a 'good' death, and we found immediate peace.

Dad was home for a little over four hours after he had died, which gave us time to speak to my brothers, sit with Dad while we ate lunch, and have a visit from Kerri-Anne and then his GP (who completed the death certificate). These hours felt incredibly precious – we're so thankful we were in our own home, away from bright lights, beeping machines and other people. There was no need to vacate the room for cleaning, and we were able to feel relaxed and unrushed. In due course, the funeral directors, who were local to our area, arrived to transport Dad to their facility, where he was to stay overnight. As upsetting as it was, and it was VERY upsetting watching him get wheeled outside and placed in the back of their van, when the time came for Dad to leave home, we were filled with relief he had died on his own terms and that we had been able to deliver his wishes. Fittingly, the funeral director left a sprig of *Acacia pycnantha* (commonly known as golden wattle) on Dad's pillow, which had always been one of his favourite flowers. We still have it and, although it was just a small thing, it was one of those beautiful little touches that made the process on the day just a little more bearable. We're also pretty sure Dad would have had an ironic laugh knowing he left the premises in a Hyundai van – he was so scathing of that vehicle make when they first arrived in Australia decades ago! It gave us all a good laugh.

Dad died on 28 November 2023, the day before his youngest grandchild's (our son's) 14th birthday. The funny thing about the date of his death is that it was EXACTLY (to the day) five years after he presented to our local hospital with a dangerously low pulse and was assessed as requiring an immediate pacemaker. That year, we celebrated our son's 9th birthday in hospital with Dad, cake and all. This time around, Dad was not with us in person for any birthday cake, but we felt his presence around us, and he was very much in our hearts and minds just the same.

Did we get it right? Yes, I believe we did

Shortly after Dad took his last breath, I rang my brothers to deliver the news. It was a challenging phone call, and we were all very upset. Although we knew the end was nigh, none of us had predicted earlier that morning that I would be calling a few hours later to tell them Dad had died. We shouldn't have been surprised, because we all knew death is unpredictable, but it was still a bit of a shock because of how quickly the last hour panned out.

I rang my brothers in age order, not for any particular reason, though I did know my eldest brother would be home between shifts, while the other would be at work. The younger of the two said to me, 'If you'd asked Dad eight years ago how he wanted the end of his life to look, he would have given you guys ten out of ten for how you've managed everything.' I was already crying, so it wasn't that comment that created the tears, but what an incredibly affirming message that was – I KNEW we had done a good job as Dad peacefully left us, I KNEW we had 'accompanied' him well and I KNEW no one else could have done a better job than those who knew Dad best. Nevertheless, hearing this from one of my siblings was so moving, and I felt very proud of all of us as a family. We live very close to the nursing home Dad was in but, even so, who knows if we would all have made it on time to see him in his last hour of life if things had progressed as they did that day. Obviously we have no way of knowing if his death would have played out any differently than it did in his home environment, but it's something that gave us great comfort afterwards – knowing our decision to bring him home and have him in the living room with us around him greatly increased the likelihood we could be there and not experience regret later for being unable to make it on time.

The next day, feeling at peace with how events had panned out, I wrote a Facebook post to announce Dad's life had come to an end. It remains a poignant summary of how we feel about the choice we made:

> As a family, we feel truly grateful for the opportunity to bring Dad home and it was an absolute honour to provide palliative care in our own environment. It felt peaceful, natural, non-threatening and right. Not everyone has the resources, opportunity or desire to contemplate their loved one dying at home, but I literally cannot put into words how grateful we are for the fact we changed our expected plan, made the choice to take Dad out of care and bring him home.

SIX

QUT Body Bequest Program

Dad made it clear to us many years ago he wanted to donate his body 'to science' at the time of his death. He was a community-minded man and a pragmatist; for him, his physical body was purely a vehicle for living life, meaning it could be of use to others when he no longer required it. This was not about leaving a legacy that would live on for many years to come although that, in fact, **is** the reality when you bequeath your body. When Mum and Dad moved interstate to live with us in 2012, Dad contacted one of the major teaching universities and completed the paperwork for body donation. Mum was aware of the details, but it wasn't really a topic of ongoing conversation – it was something we knew would be coming our way at some point, that required no further attention for now.

When it became clear we were edging closer to the end of Dad's life, we felt it was prudent to pull out the paperwork, contact the university and start some preliminary conversations. Mum made the initial phone call and reported back to me when I returned home later that morning. It turned out the facility was about to undergo a renovation and may not, in fact, be available to us in the timeframe we expected we may require it. There was also no guarantee Dad would fit their admission criteria, which felt confronting for Mum when our focus was to grant Dad his wish. However, perhaps the woman on the phone picked up on her disappointment and confusion about what that would mean for us moving forwards because, right at the end of the phone call, the lady mentioned to Mum there may be another alternative for Dad and provided the phone number for the QUT Body Bequest Program.

Mum had already rung the coordinator by the time I arrived home, and she was feeling good about both the potential change of venue and the suitability of the program for Dad. Knowing me as she does, Mum assumed I would have questions of my own and suggested I speak to the coordinator myself to satisfy my own mind. She knows me well! I rang him straight back that afternoon and was overwhelmed by the kindness and respect he expressed for Dad's wishes. After a great chat, I knew immediately we were in the right place and felt 100% assured that the research, education and training for health professionals their program offers would be exactly how Dad would want to be involved. That evening, I read a fabulous article about their program, forwarded it to my brothers and completed the necessary paperwork for Dad to enter the QUT Body Bequest Program. I was confident there should be no foreseeable reason we could not follow through with Dad's intention.

Just as there had been on the day Dad arrived home, there were some serendipitous connections between the coordinator of the Body Bequest Program and our family – not only did he have his own personal connection with dementia, but he also lived in a neighbouring suburb and actually used to live in our street! Can you believe it? Crazy. Once again, everything felt 'just as it was meant to be', and it was comforting to know there was a familiarity for the person whose care Dad would enter after his death. The coordinator also mentioned it was highly likely the surgeon who inserted Dad's pacemaker would have come through their facility for ongoing education of some kind during the last 10 years. I had this feeling of things somehow going 'full circle'.

One of the most welcome things about the Body Bequest Program is how streamlined and non-demanding the process is.

Having completed the paperwork in advance of Dad's death, it meant everything was in place for 'when the time came' and there was nothing further to do. On the day Dad died, when we felt ready to say our final goodbyes, we simply contacted the funeral director to advise them of his death and the rest was taken care of by them. As you read in the previous chapter, Dad stayed in their facility overnight and was then moved to QUT the following morning. I received a phone call from the coordinator upon his arrival, so we knew Dad was in safe hands from that point on and that we had delivered him another of his long-term wishes.

A few months after his death, we received our invitation to the Body Bequest Program's annual Thanksgiving and Remembrance Ceremony. Mum and I were thrilled we could be there, along with an old family friend who has known both Mum and Dad since they were all teenagers. It was an emotionally-charged morning, and a true reflection of the beauty and respect offered by the program itself:

- The string quartet that welcomed guests and played during and after the ceremony was an immediate 'trigger' for me, in terms of feeling an instant connection to Dad.

- Most of the magnificent floral arrangements adorning the venue were natives, Dad's absolute favourite flowers.

- The food offered for morning tea was presented beautifully, which our easily pleased and down-to-earth Dad would certainly have described as 'fancy'!

As well as a beautifully scribed book listing all donors from the previous twelve months, one of the things available for families to read on the day was 'notes of thanks' from ten different students who passed through the program as part of their medical studies. I have not reproduced them all here, but I am including a few to give an impression of the value these students derived from their experience of hands-on learning. As you can imagine, these were extremely moving messages for us to read that day, and we'll always remember how they made us feel:

- *Dear Family of Donor. I am exceedingly grateful for the opportunity your loved one offered me. I can imagine it must have been a big sacrifice, but I hope you find comfort in knowing that their donation not only furthered my learning but also the future of medicine and science. I thank you for your generosity, I believe I have learnt invaluable lessons and gained significant knowledge from your loved one's donation. I thank you so much. An anatomy student.*

- *To the Donor – From a blessed student. I could not be any more privileged to be able to give you a second life, although you may no longer move or have a voice, what you have given to the world is one of the most valuable things anyone could offer, "knowledge". I am incredibly blessed to be able to learn, to empathise and to give you a second life to further help many others. May you rest in peace knowing that you are a part of the creation of a brighter future. Thank you, A future anatomist.*

- *Thank you. The opportunity to learn from your loved one's donation has been invaluable to me. It has both furthered my medical education and given me a profound insight into the miracle of life. This opportunity has instilled in me a sense of responsibility and I am now walking away from this experience knowing that I put my very best into this to do you justice and make you proud. An anatomy student.*

- *Dear Donor. Thank you for this amazing life-changing opportunity that has fuelled my drive to be a doctor, but it has given me a new appreciation for life, and the human body. I am much more conscious of the life choices I make and realise the fragility and importance of the body I am in. So, thank you again for kindness, trust and selflessness. I will never forget. A future doctor.*

Basking in the warmth of what had been a beautiful morning for us, that night I wrote the following Facebook post. It sums up perfectly how we felt after the service and the significance of sharing our family's experience of body donation with others:

Today we had the wonderful opportunity to attend the QUT Thanksgiving and Remembrance Ceremony, put on every year by the university's Body Bequest Program. The theatre was packed with family and friends of those who had donated their bodies during 2023. We heard from a range of speakers associated with research, training and education via the Body Bequest Program, including two surgeons, a lecturer and a paramedic. Each one of them spoke with such respect, thanks and gratitude for both donors, and their families, and there was a definite 'vibe' in the room of shared connection.

In addition to the insights we gained about the far-reaching benefits of the program for students, health professionals, researchers and the wider community, we also heard from the daughter of one of last year's donors, who delivered a powerful reflection of her father and his enrolment into the Body Bequest Program. Truly beautiful listening, and also highly emotional.

For me, one of the highlights of the morning was meeting the program's coordinator, who is the point of contact for donor families and friends. He is a special kind of person and does his job in a special kind of way – a fact which was echoed by each of the speakers today. When I first spoke to him in the months leading up to Dad's death, I mentioned that I had written a book about our family's experience with Dad's dementia. Having his own personal story, he asked me at a later stage how he could obtain a copy of the book. Today I got the opportunity to gift him a signed copy, my small way of saying 'Thank you for looking after my dad with such love, compassion and respect'.

Contemplating body donation is certainly not for everyone, and it is not my intention to suggest it is. There are a host of cultural, spiritual, personal and other reasons why this option is not a consideration for thousands of people who die every year, and that will always be the case. What I really want to convey is the gift Dad's decision to donate his body delivered US, and the ongoing gift it will deliver others in terms of ongoing education and training for the professionals who access the program as time goes by. It is a legacy Dad would be proud of, and one several people I know are now considering for themselves at the time of their death. When feeding back to one of my brothers how fabulous the service had been, he sent the following text: 'Gee that all looks and sounds fantastic. Good call, Bob Twigg. And then good call his wife and daughter! I am sure Dad would be smugly pleased with all that and have a sense of "I told you so" about him. Wonderful. I look forwards to hearing all about it from Mum.' Yep, Dad probably did feel smug, I reckon. For years he told us body donation was the right choice for him at the time of his death, and now he had been proven correct! Again!

SEVEN

Marking the occasion with love, laughter and memories

As you read in the previous chapter, body donation meant we had no funeral to organise after Dad died, and we chose not to have a memorial service at that time either. It felt like a real bonus! It delivered an unexpected feeling of relaxation, giving us all the time in the world to hunker down as a family and celebrate Dad's life together with no time commitments, no stress, no external pressure, no invitations and no expectations. My brothers and their partners arrived and, barring a few trips out for coffee or groceries and a visit from the friend who had accompanied Mum and me to the Thanksgiving and Remembrance Ceremony, we engaged very little with the outside world for that week or so. It was a special period for all of us – a time we will always cherish. We were the people who knew Dad best, who could support each other best and who could best identify what things were going to be the most helpful to do.

So, what **did** we do to celebrate Dad's life and honour his legacy?

- We had a 'Bobathon' – over dinner one night, we all had an opportunity to share our favourite memories of Dad, any significant quotes, memorable funny experiences and so on. We knew Dad would have wanted us to enjoy our time together and have a laugh about our funny memories of him. We also knew he would understand we were feeling sad and already missing him, but that he wouldn't want us to wallow in self-pity or remember him only as he was at the very end of his long life. Plenty of tears and laughter were on offer during that meal, I can tell you!

- We had beautiful floral arrangements on the tables – not only to reflect Dad's love for native flora, but also in recognition of his involvement with various biosphere and Landcare Australia projects over his lifetime.

- Dad's famous green hat, which he was synonymous with, was always on a chair nearby, just as it had been since the moment he came out of the nursing home.

- We took a picnic to the spot we had last taken Dad, which was also where he had gone in his first ever wheelchair taxi ride when everyone visited from interstate a couple of months earlier. Hilariously, a huge storm came out of nowhere not long after we had arrived and set up our picnic. It truly felt like Dad had turned on an industrial-sized fan to show us he was there too! In fact, it was so windy we had to pack up and head back home almost immediately. Dad and his sense of humour – he certainly got the last laugh on that occasion.

- We took phone calls and read cards and messages from a wide range of people wishing to express their sympathy at Dad's passing. Some were donating funds to Dementia Australia, and all were offering their own reflections on the kind of person Dad was and the way he would be remembered. Some of the most touching messages came via our old hometown's Facebook page, and the words of those we had grown up with offered our family enormous comfort at that time. As I said in an earlier chapter, technology has its downsides and I'm not a huge fan of social media. But, in this context, reconnecting with people who had known Mum and Dad for decades and now wished to share their memories was very moving. In that sense, it was like a private memorial service with the opportunity for input from others, but only open to close family members.

- As a family, we paid a visit to Dad's nursing home. We wanted to express our thanks to staff who had cared for him, some for more than two years, and also to say our goodbyes. As expected, it was an emotional visit, particularly for Mum, who had come to know some of the other residents and also their family members. It was always going to be confronting returning there without Dad, especially walking out past his room, but it was something we wanted to do, and it felt like a 'milestone' reached once we had done it.

- We looked at lots and lots of photos, particularly those that showed Dad with his two youngest grandchildren (our kids) after he and Mum moved in with us in 2012. As is always the case immediately after a loss, the photographic memories did bring tears and sadness, but they also brought huge smiles, guffaws of laughter and warmth to our hearts as we felt Dad around us.

Once everyone had gone

The last of the family visitors left just over two weeks before Christmas. Mum decided she would fly interstate and spend time with my eldest brother and his partner over Christmas and into the New Year, something we had been encouraging her to contemplate after Dad's death. While she was there, and in honour of his fondness for particular trees, they planted a *Hakea laurina*, a beautiful native that hails from the southwestern region of Australia. It's growing like wildfire and is a living legacy to Dad.

My husband was rostered to work over the Christmas to New Year period, so the kids and I retreated into the Queensland outback to join him. I was ready to 'decompress' after what had been a very intense six months, and it was time to replenish my soul and experience the restorative nature of open space, red dirt, summer storms, isolation, peace and quiet. I gave the kids 'driving lessons' (they are underage; don't tell anyone!), I cooked, we played board games and we 'worked out' with weights, tennis racquets and skipping ropes. It was fabulous and just what I needed to reflect, regroup and reset for the year ahead. On Christmas Day, one of only a handful I have ever spent without both my parents, and obviously the first one since Dad's death, I missed wishing him a merry Christmas and seeing him in his Santa hat. But I felt his spirit around us that day and knew he would always be there. Thankfully, that sense continues to this day, and I never really feel without him as I travel around our local area – years of memories abound and they reside at the favourite picnic spots, the dog beach, along the waterfront and so on. Even now, there are still times I find myself glancing over to see if Dad is sitting outside the supermarket waiting for Mum, exactly where I found him many times in the days he lived at home. As my brother said, old memories run deep.

Final resting place

The time will come when we can take Dad back to his spiritual home of Western Australia, where he spent just over 50 years of his life and where the three of us (myself and my brothers) grew up. We will lay him to rest in our hometown, something we are all very much looking forward to, and I reckon we'll have a meal and a drink at the pub afterwards. His ashes will be given to us once his 'work' at the university is complete, and he will then 'retire' from community service once and for all. However, his legacy will live on in the two books I have now written about him, the speaking events I will be part of moving forwards and the future work opportunities I intend to carve out for myself. In the words of Jack Thorne, 'Those we love never truly leave us. There are things that death cannot touch.'

EIGHT

Advance care planning and getting your affairs in order

Prior to Dad being diagnosed with dementia more than six years ago, Mum and Dad's preparedness for end of life was limited to the existence of his will, the appointment of me as enduring power of attorney, conversations about not being kept alive when quality of life was absent and, as you have already read, body donation. That was about it. Some people are more prepared, but the vast majority are even less prepared – according to Palliative Care CEO Violet Platt, 'Over 90% of us know that we should have these conversations, but less than 40% of us do.'[6]

So, what is advance care planning?

Advance care planning is much more than just having a current will, though many of us haven't even taken that most basic of steps, let alone any others on the forward planning path. As the name suggests, advance care planning is literally 'planning in advance' of ill health and/or death:

> Advance care planning involves planning for your future health care. It enables you to make some decisions now about

---

6. https://www.abc.net.au/listen/programs/lifematters/have-you-talked-to-your-loved-one-about-their-end-of-life-choice/103545296

the health care you would or would not like to receive if you were to become seriously ill and unable to communicate your preferences or make treatment decisions.

Advance care planning gives you the opportunity to think about, discuss and record your preferences for the type of care you would like to receive and the outcomes you would consider acceptable.

Advance care planning helps to ensure your loved ones and health providers know what matters most to you and respect your treatment preferences.

Ideally, advance care planning will result in your preferences being documented in a plan known as an advance care directive and the appointment of a substitute decision maker to help ensure your preferences are respected.[7]

My husband and I have had a will for many years. We have always had documentation about care arrangements for our children should something happen to both of us, and we've known each other's wishes regarding organ donation. Prior to the journey we were on with Dad over the last few years, that was about the extent of any formalised advance care planning in our household, though we are now a lot more organised and prepared! By the end of this chapter, I hope I will have encouraged you to actively engage with the process of advance care planning, regardless of your age or your current health status, if you haven't already done so. It's never too early.

---

7. https://www.advancecareplanning.org.au/understand-advance-care-planning/advance-care-planning-explained

The kinds of things we should be thinking about and discussing with our loved ones

This is not an exhaustive list by any means, but the following questions might help you get started:

- Do you have a current will? Does it include statements about guardianship of your children if something happens to you?

- Has anyone in your life been appointed as an enduring power of attorney for personal and health-related issues? What about financial decision-making? Or will this be handled by the state?

- Have you identified a substitute decision maker for if/when you can no longer make decisions yourself? Is guardianship required?

- Have you completed an Advance Health Directive, Advanced Care Directive and/or Statement of Choices? Does it include specific details about prolonging your life? Resuscitation? Ventilation? Supplementation of nutrients/ food/hydration? Tube feeding (either nasogastric or gastrostomy)? IV drips? Antibiotics? Surgery? Blood transfusions?

- Is your preferred place of death known to your loved ones – home, hospice, hospital, nursing home?

- If you have one, have you spoken to your health care team about your wishes? Are they available to support you? What would that look like, in terms of ongoing treatment, medications, referral to services and availability? What about provision of personal care?

- What's your 'best-case scenario' in terms of how your death looks? Who is present? Kids? Pets? Music? Do you have preferences around pain relief? Are there religious, cultural or spiritual practices to consider?

- Do loved ones know your wishes in terms of a funeral, memorial service, celebration of life, burial, cremation? Have you prepaid any of the expenses related to these options and told a loved one the details?

- If donation is relevant to you, are you registered with a brain bank? Body bequest program? Organ and/or tissue donation service? There is no time to lose in these situations, so discussion and forward planning is preferable.

- Do your loved ones know where to find information pertaining to all the above, as well as bank account details, superannuation, life insurance, real estate, investments etc.? Is there a legacy contact person for your social media accounts?

It might seem like a lot to think about, or perhaps it seems too confronting to give much thought to. It can be hard to imagine the need for such complex decision-making (especially when you feel 'too young') if you are in good health, with nothing to suggest illness or an accident is coming your way.

So maybe it's easier to think about future planning in terms of your loved ones left behind after your death. Or to imagine them being forced into making decisions about your care because you no longer have capacity to do so, and they don't know what you would have wanted them to do. That can be a very heavy burden to carry, and people feel the weight of those responsibilities keenly – I've seen it in critical care settings, both personally and professionally. So, while we can't plan for every eventuality, nor foresee what might happen to us and when, we can keep our affairs in order and future plan for the 'best-case scenario'. Hopefully, that will avoid, or at least reduce, the impact on our loved ones of making decisions they THINK might be in our best interest, or in line with our wishes, at an already challenging time. On the Advance Care Planning Australia website (https://www.advancecareplanning.org.au) there is a series of thought-provoking videos that play out various case studies. One shows two brothers talking after one of them was required to make a decision about resuscitating the other when he was in an unconscious state. It's an interesting watch.

Is advance care planning different for those living with dementia?

Advance care planning takes on a whole new importance when you consider it in terms of diseases that affect neurological capacity. When Dad's definitive dementia diagnosis was finally given, we quickly realised we needed to formalise his wishes about future treatments and interventions while he still had the capacity to articulate them. We arranged for an advance care planning nurse to come to the house, and she sat down with Mum, Dad and me to complete the relevant paperwork, recording his future wishes. At the time, Dad was living at home and still very much engaged in normal family life. Yes, he was no longer driving, and we were seeing more and more behaviours consistent with an expected dementia trajectory, but his quality of life was very much intact and he was able to make his wishes known. Time was really of the essence though, and I'm glad we took advice and didn't delay doing the relevant paperwork:

> Promotion of individual autonomy and respecting the person's wishes when capacity is failing or lost is paramount and can be best achieved by early planning. As such the promotion of advance care planning in the early stage of dementia, or even earlier, will help facilitate care that is in keeping with the person's wishes and values and facilitates decision making for families.[8]

Given that none of us know if or when we may be affected by a neurological disease, or any other scenario that threatens or even ends our life, we should all be talking about this topic and taking early action to make plans for ill health and death.

---

8. Dementia Australia Paper Number 43 (prepared in collaboration with Palliative Care Australia), 2017

How did future planning documentation and previous conversations about quality of life assist us when we were making decisions about Dad's care, particularly as the end of his life was drawing closer?

As stated above, with an advance care planning nurse, Dad had formalised his wishes (and they had been uploaded on the state health department database), and we knew where he stood on various issues. Based on conversations we had with him over the years, we knew his beliefs, his values and what was important to him as a person. This made making any care decisions, particularly as we got closer to the end of his life, a whole lot easier and ensured we were not carrying the burden of feeling uncertain about his wishes:

Will – this had been in place for many years, with some updates, long before dementia was part of our family story.

Enduring power of attorney (EPoA) paperwork – even before Dad's diagnosis, I had been appointed EPoA for personal, health and financial decisions. By the way, it is super important your EPoA understands your value base and what's important to you in life, as well as what your wishes are as they pertain to medical interventions, treatment and care at the end of your life. While an EPoA may never need to do anything, if they do need to make personal, health and/ or financial decisions on your behalf, you need to feel confident they would be able to accurately relay what your beliefs were and what your wishes would have been.

Pacemaker – at the time this was recommended, Dad still had good quality of life and we wanted his life to continue. Although his understanding of the need for a pacemaker, and what was involved with the procedure, was already compromised by his cognitive decline by then, we would never have argued against it being implanted. Instead, we focussed on maximising the comfort of his hospital stay to make it happen.

Hip surgery – had Dad's hip been broken as a result of a fall, we were in agreement we would not consider hip surgery for him as he was in the advanced stage of dementia by that time. Although he had still been able to enjoy going out with us, coming home for lunch, going for walks etc., his quality of life was already significantly compromised, and that would have been worse if he had been recovering from hip surgery. As agreed with the treating doctor at the time, we felt ongoing pain relief, physiotherapy and referral to the community liaison team was the optimal way forward.

Antibiotics – As you read in Chapter 2, I only realised the issue of antibiotics was not 'clear-cut' in my own mind when I was in the back of an ambulance with Dad, enroute to hospital, after there were concerns he had aspirated. He certainly did not have capacity for making medical decisions by that late stage so, had they been suggested (which they weren't), responsibility for deciding whether to fill the script and administer any treatment would have fallen to me, in consultation with my husband and Mum. I'm still not 100% sure what I would have done in that situation – on the one hand, I may have chosen not to intervene and potentially shortened Dad's life. On the other hand, I knew Mum probably wasn't yet ready to say goodbye to Dad and also that my brothers would be arriving soon from interstate. As I said earlier, it was a stark reminder of how even the clearest of wishes can feel uncertain when you are in the moment and your emotions are heightened.

Eating and drinking – As independent feeding got harder and harder for Dad to manage, there was an increasing need to cut up his food and assist him with eating and drinking. Although his wishes pertaining to these things had not been specifically set out in planning documents, we took Dad's lead and simply accepted when he seemed to have had enough, was 'playing' with his food with no obvious intention of eating it or, sometimes, actually verbalised he didn't want whatever was being offered. There was a level of comfort (for us) in assisting Dad to eat his meals on those occasions when it appeared he was enjoying us doing so. I guess it was another way to demonstrate our love and care for him, and these opportunities were slowly dwindling away. As you read in Chapter 4, by the time we decided to bring Dad home, he was well down the path of non-life-sustaining intake of food and fluids, and we would never have considered any method of artificial feeding or hydration prior to that. Interestingly enough, during this time, Mum recalled a conversation Dad had with a friend many years earlier (well before dementia was a topic) when he had made it clear he would simply stop eating and drinking if he had no quality of life and was ready to die. Although he was now in the advanced stage of dementia, and assumed to be unable to make such conscious choices about this issue, perhaps he was exercising his ultimate right, just as he had said he would all those years ago? Obviously, a reduced interest in eating and drinking is a natural indicator of end of life approaching, so perhaps that's really what it was. Either way, the recall of that conversation was reassuring for us – it provided some comfort as we contemplated Dad's choices, and the things we knew had always been important for him at the end of his life.

Resuscitation and ventilation – Dad's wishes were that neither of these interventions would be used in the absence of quality of life. Obviously, we never needed to make any decisions around resuscitation or ventilation but, if we had been required to, his wishes were clear and would have confidently directed us along the path of comfort care only (pain and symptoms well managed) so that nature could take its course.

Place of death – as you read in Chapter 4, we acted on our belief that Dad's wish was to come home to die. At the time he completed his planning paperwork, we assumed he would likely die in hospital from a respiratory illness, and Dad indicated he would have been happy with that outcome. When this wasn't the case, and a natural death was looming, we did what we were sure would have been preferable for him and took him back into our own care.

Body bequest – as you read in Chapter 6, the relevant paperwork was done prior to Dad's death, with a backup plan for cremation if body donation was somehow unavailable. I'm very glad we 'checked in' with the original university as Dad's condition was rapidly deteriorating and discovered this option was going to be unavailable to us; otherwise, we may well have missed the opportunity to carry out his wish for body donation.

Helpful resources for advance care planning

In Australia, paperwork and terminology around advance care planning varies slightly from state to state, so it's worth familiarising yourself with the relevant documentation in your area, and potentially uploading health and care-related planning paperwork to your medical record and/or the state health database. These national resources are a good starting point:

www.advancecareplanning.org.au

All things advance care planning – this is an excellent, Australia-specific website (although there are similar organisations in different countries). It includes guidelines for the issues you might like to consider when creating advance care plans, as well as resources and videos for opening up conversations and much more.

www.end-of-life.qut.edu.au

All things end-of-life law – once again, this is Australia-specific and provides up-to-date information on a range of topics including capacity and consent, palliative medication, assisted dying, withholding treatment and more.

**www.health.gov.au/topics/palliative-care/
planning-your-palliative-care/advance-care-planning**

This is the Australian Government's Department of Health and Aged Care website, which contains easy-to-understand advance care planning information.

https://www.digitalhealth.gov.au/initiatives-and-programs/my-health-record

This is effectively a 'digital health' folder, provided by the Australian Government. Advance care planning documentation can be uploaded to your 'My Health Record', where it can be accessed by medical staff (your GP and hospital staff) if you are not able to verbally explain your wishes.

Depending on where in the world you are reading this book, there will be different services available to you that deal specifically with advance care planning in your home area. I encourage you to take the time to find out what those services are and engage with the process of advance care planning before time is against you, or before your loved one with dementia loses capacity.

And now for something different (but also a little bit the same)

While I was undertaking research for this book, I happened upon Marie Alessi[9] – TEDx and keynote speaker, MC for Celebrations of Life, facilitator for workshop and family bereavement sessions, and podcaster. I was fascinated by her inspiring story, not only how she found empowerment in an excruciatingly dreadful situation (the sudden, unexpected death of her soulmate and life partner, Rob), but how she has since helped thousands of others on their journey to healing grief. I reached out to Marie for a chat and, with her permission, I am sharing a summary of her story below. Although from an advance care planning 'paperwork' point of view Rob and Marie were unprepared for the end of his life (no will, no EPoA, no health directives, nothing), it's such a beautiful story that I feel compelled to share it with you:

Less than three years before Rob died, he took a detour on his way from work one night due to a fatal accident. Later that night, they

---

9. www.mariealessi.com

learnt it was a young father who had been killed, the result of being hit by a truck front-on. This prompted Marie and Rob to have the 'what if' conversation. They didn't know it at the time, but perhaps the most significant thing they shared that night was, 'If something was to ever happen to me, I would want you to create the happiest life possible for you and the boys!' At that time, they were completely unaware of the impact this conversation would have on Marie's life, as well as the lives of their two young boys.

Fast forward almost three years, and Marie's world was turned upside down by a phone call from the coroner's office – while on the other side of the country for work, Rob had suffered a brain aneurysm and died instantly. It's impossible for me to imagine receiving this phone call. As she hugged her boys and told them the news, she heard Rob's words from the night of the 'what if' conversation. Marie had no idea at the time how to make this promise come true, yet happiness became her North Star.

So began Marie's journey into writing, creating a safe space for others who were grieving, sharing her story globally, exploring a different approach to grief and assisting others to celebrate life. Her approach is refreshing, and her 'vibe' is warm and positive. She is truly embracing Rob's wishes, though not in a medical way – these are his beliefs, his values, his personal wishes for her and their boys. And these are equally important to understand in your loved ones – we simply don't know what might be lurking around the corner.

In summary

I did an advance care training workshop with end-of-life doula Jacqui Williams[10] and her five key points to summarise advance care planning really stuck with me:

1. **Think** – what's important to you in terms of future planning for the end of your life? What would happen if you became

---

10. www.endoflifetransitions.com.au

seriously ill, had an accident or were suddenly diagnosed with a terminal illness?

2. **Learn** – research your options and what the consequences/outcomes of those options might be.

3. **Decide** – what are your preferences, what needs to be included and what might help your loved ones make decisions about your care if/when the time arises?

4. **Talk** – who are the people who will be making decisions on your behalf or need to know your wishes? Have conversations with them so they are aware of your preferences.

5. **Record** – document your wishes by completing the relevant paperwork.

Just as the need for palliative care increases over time, so too will the significance of advance care planning. Have conversations with your loved ones NOW about palliative and end-of-life wishes while they are still able to articulate their thoughts, give consent and complete paperwork. Addressing these matters ahead of time gives everyone confidence their wishes will be respected in the event they become sick or no longer have capacity. If there is only one thing you take from this book, I hope it is this message and that you spread the word to your friends and family to do the same. Confidence comes from preparedness and, ultimately, that's what will allow you to maintain some semblance of control over your future.

NINE

The personal, and professional, growth continues

I have been on a massive learning curve over the last few years, not only as our family navigated Dad's dementia and sought to accompany him through the dying process in the most dignified and peaceful manner, but also since. As well as having now written two books (something I NEVER expected to do), perhaps the most positive outcome of this years-long journey for me has been the opportunity I have had to educate myself and upskill in many areas. I am keen to keep learning and explore new work opportunities, and I've become even more motivated to share our family's story and hear from others about theirs. This has all developed as a direct result of my personal experiences with Dad.

As we've traversed the palliative dementia space, I've found myself discussing death cafés, brain banks, end-of-life celebrations, cooling beds, green burials, morphine, death walkers, clean grief, water cremations and much more. I've presented our family story to community groups and meetings, undertaken courses, attended workshops, read books, googled (a lot!), spoken to those in the field, listened to podcasts (and appeared on a couple as a guest), and accepted an invitation to speak about our end-of-life experience at an international dementia conference later this year. I am very grateful for the resources and expertise I have been able to access and consider myself so fortunate for how generously people have shared their time and wisdom with me.

So, aside from learning a whole lot about the language around palliative care and what is important at end of life:

- What else have I learnt?
- What are some of my takeaway messages from the last few years?
- And how can I, as a community member, 'do my bit' to increase death literacy and encourage conversations about dying?

Let's touch on what have been some of my biggest learnings.

Palliative care is not just about cancer or imminent death, and is not just the domain of specialist services

As I said in Chapter 1, palliative care is largely misunderstood in the wider community, with three of the incorrect assumptions being that it:

- relates purely to specific diseases (particularly cancer)
- means death is imminent
- is purely the domain of specialists.

While specialised services grew out of a need identified towards the end of last century to provide expertise in the area of cancer care, there is a growing requirement to educate the community and 'reshape' society's expectations around palliative care. As per the World Health Organization:

> Specialist palliative care is one component of palliative care service delivery. But a sustainable, quality and accessible palliative care system needs to be integrated into primary health

care, community and home-based care, as well as support-ing care providers such as family and community volunteers. Providing palliative care should be considered an ethical duty for health professionals.[11]

There is little doubt that specialist palliative care services provide well for families who can access them. For the father of one of my friends, referral to his local service was a positive experience as his cancer journey came peacefully to an end – the service was free, all-inclusive and immediate, meaning the family felt well supported, they were able to care for their dad at home with professional nursing input each day and they knew what to expect as the end of his life approached. The simple fact is that existing specialist palliative care services:

- are inadequate for our ageing population
- will be unable to deliver the volume of care we need for dignified dying into the future
- often have long wait times, and hence tight referral and prioritisation criteria
- are often difficult to access in regional and remote areas.

What does this mean for us as a society as we live longer with chronic disease, terminal illnesses and progressive neurological conditions? I am particularly interested in this as it relates to dementia, given pro-jections for its prevalence into the future (more than 812,500 people living with dementia by 2054).[12] As stated in Chapter 1, specialist palliative care services are not necessarily required for people living with dementia unless they have additional complex medical needs; however, high-quality palliative and end-of-life services certainly are.

The concept of building 'compassionate communities' has become core business for palliative care organisations across the globe as they seek to educate the wider population (including GPs, aged care staff,

---

11. https://www.who.int/news-room/fact-sheets/detail/palliative-care
12. https:// www.dementia.org.au/about-dementia/dementia-facts-and-figures

acute setting workers, community carers, family members and volunteers) about:

- managing life-limiting illnesses
- what to expect from death
- how to prepare for dying
- the needs of the bereaved.

But what does 'compassionate communities' even mean? Put simply, it's about creating supportive, well-connected communities, upskilling generalist services and increasing society's capacity (as a whole) to deliver care, promote quality of life and facilitate dignified death. It is widely discussed that there is a need for a rapid expansion of services for the dying in the community as we seek to support a growing number of people requiring care. As family members and future carers, we must be part of advocating for more resources, as well as working together to use the ones currently available to us, both within the public system and within our own neighbourhoods. But, perhaps even more importantly, we really must educate ourselves (and our families, friends and colleagues) as to how we can adequately access high-quality palliative and end-of-life care for our loved ones.

Given that many of the needs of those in palliative care or at end of life are non-clinical needs, supportive communities can (and already do) offer much of what is being provided by specialist services. For example, a person with complex symptoms may be well managed by their treating health care team in consultation with a specialist palliative care team. On 20 May 2024, during Palliative Care Week 2024, Palliative Care Australia posted the following statement on their Facebook page, and it effectively highlights the concept of a 'community' approach:

> Palliative care can be delivered by general practitioners, registered nurses, nurse practitioners, allied health professionals, aged care workers, volunteers and carers, as well as

specialist palliative care services. They all play a critical role in delivering exceptional care and optimising quality of life.

Given that some of the needs of people living with dementia are unique, training specific to the delivery of high-quality palliative care for them must be a priority, not only within the aged care sector, but across mainstream primary and community-based services. As you will read below, there is room to improve in that space, and we must strive to do so. The growing role of the dementia doula is an innovative part of the solution, as they educate the community about the disease and also provide ongoing support, including palliative and end-of-life care, to those living with dementia and their families.

If you are interested in learning more about the concept of compassionate communities and how you can 'play your part', you might be interested in the following websites:

www.compassionatecommunities.au

www.thegroundswellproject.com/compassionate-communities

www.palliativecarewa.asn.au/carers-and-families/compassionate-communities/

End-of-life care is not always well understood, even within the health and aged care sectors

As I've set about recounting our story and seeking input from others, it's become very clear to me that palliative and end-of-life experiences don't always deliver positive outcomes for those dying and/or their loved ones left behind. While exercising choice and facilitating Dad's wishes worked very well for our family, I have heard several stories where things have gone wrong and the outcome has been far from peaceful – some from within nursing homes, some from within the hospital setting and some from home death scenarios.

A friend recently opened up to me about her mother's end-of-life experience two years ago, a scenario that was so traumatic for her that she has now commenced therapy to process the outstanding grief she is still struggling with all this time later. Her mum was living in residential care during the advanced stages of dementia when she suffered a heart attack one night and was transferred to a large public hospital. My friend recounted how she and her mum had had many conversations over the years about her mother's wishes for end of life, and she assumed she would be well placed to liaise with treating staff when the time came to facilitate a dignified and timely death for her. The reality, however, was far from peaceful, and she was deeply affected by it.

As she was driving to the hospital to be with her mother that night, my friend took a call from an emergency department doctor seeking consent for anaesthesia and the insertion of a stent (a mesh tube used to hold open narrow spaces such as blood vessels) into her mum's artery. She was confused by his unexpected phone call, given the planning her mum had done about end-of-life decision-making, and was shocked to feel pressured (over the phone, while driving) into making a decision to prolong her mum's life after a heart attack. Given she was not far away, she managed to delay consenting to any intervention and expected the matter would be quickly resolved with further discussion about her mum's wishes upon her arrival at the hospital. Instead, she found herself feeling guilty and unsure as she contemplated not giving consent for any such procedure and instead advocating (against the doctor's recommendation) on behalf of her mother to refuse treatment and, ultimately, die. Although her advanced dementia meant she could no longer comprehend the medical situation herself, my friend knew this would have been her mother's wish by that stage of her life and that she would have wanted her to make this decision on her behalf. However, she still felt pressured and doubted herself. Fortunately, a more experienced doctor joined the conversation at a critical time and gave my friend 'permission' to 'just say no' to requests for an unnecessary procedure and unwanted treatment so that her mum could move towards a natural death. Reflecting on the relief she had felt at finally being heard that night, my friend made the following comment:

> What if I'd caved to the pressure I was feeling from the treating doctor and said yes to the procedure? Would we have had more time with Mum (assuming she didn't die because of the anaesthetic)? Maybe, but I didn't want more time with her as she was at that stage in her life. She was tormented and paranoid, it was terrible to watch. All this from someone who had always made it clear to her family that she didn't want to continue living if her cognition was affected, that she didn't want to just 'hang on to life' when quality was no longer there.

Hearing my friend recount their family's situation was very sad for two reasons:

- the immense pressure she felt to make a quick decision which she knew (had she said yes) would go against what her mother had always said she wanted

- honouring her mother's wishes and saying 'no' opposed the treating doctor's advice and, thanks to the seed of doubt he planted, this meant she second-guessed herself. This resulted in significant guilt (not only at the time of her mum's hospitalisation, but many times since) as to whether she did the right thing in denying her mum treatment. Her heart knows she has, but her head still asks the question.

Unfortunately for my friend, the 'less than ideal' end-of-life scenario continued, and it took three days for her mum to be moved onto a palliative care ward where the focus could move to a pain-free, dignified death. After a long stay in emergency, she was first admitted to a medical ward shared with three other people and staff who did not seem to have the skills, training or capacity to cater for the needs of a dying dementia patient. With a total lack of privacy and an ongoing feeling of uncertainty around an expected timeframe for her mother's pending death, my friend and her family did their best to provide comfort and reassurance that everything would be okay and to tentatively say goodbye. When she was finally transferred to a palliative care ward and into a room of her own, the situation began to calm, a sense of control was restored and her mum slipped peacefully away.

So, what might be 'getting in the way' of best-practice decisions in the hospital setting?

- Is there, at times, too much emphasis on saving a patient's life (which we have become very good at, thanks to the advancement of medications and technology), perhaps to the detriment of the individual? As in my friend's case, advanced dementia patients are a good example of when life-prolonging interventions may, in fact, be completely inappropriate, and comfort care should be the focus.

- My friend found it hard to be heard that night. Is there sometimes a 'dismissive' attitude to the family's knowledge of a situation; an assumption that they don't understand the medical consequences of denying intervention and treatment? Once again, in her case, this led to a confronting exchange with the treating doctor as she spoke on behalf of her mother and what she knew her wishes to be. Thank goodness she slowed the process down, challenged the doctor's opinion and advocated on behalf of her mum.

- Is there simply a lack of palliative care and end-of-life training in the medical curriculum? Do we just assume all health care staff know how to identify, treat and respect the wishes of a dying patient? As you will read below, it is known that existing palliative care services will not be able to cater for our future needs moving forwards. We must increase understanding and awareness around palliative and end-of-life care, not only across the health sector as a whole, but also within the wider community.

So, what about the aged care sector? Given we began the process of moving Dad back home with us 12 days before he died, we never fully explored how end-of-life care would have looked if he had remained at his nursing home. Curious to understand this more, I sat down with the facility's care manager a few months after Dad died and asked her what we could have expected, as death got closer, if he had still been a resident. She explained that their site promotes maximum family involvement in death and prides itself on how they manage end-of-life care for their residents. She confirmed:

- We would have been able to stay with Dad 24 hours a day, with meals and support from staff offered to us as required.

- Dad would have been monitored for pain on a constant basis, with a move to a syringe driver only if/when this was required.

While that sounds like a promising benchmark for a proactive, involved family, like ours always was, I also wanted to know how end-of-life care looks for the 15% of people in their facility who either don't have family involved at all, or have family who are not able to be there for a whole host of different reasons. The care manager reiterated that they see their residents as being like family, regardless of how long they have lived on site, and therefore treat them as family when they move towards the end of their lives. As a mark of respect, and to preserve dignity for a dying resident, she confirmed no one would be on their own as they approached death, and no one would suffer or experience pain, as the focus would be on comfort and companionship. I commented to her that, sadly, in talking to a number of carers since Dad's death, I had heard negative experiences about end-of-life care in some nursing homes – including a general lack of skills, training and understanding of high-quality care; poor communication between facility and family members (particularly around timeframes for anticipated death); poor knowledge of symptom management; and a lack of support for families/partners wishing to 'companion' their loved ones into death. She conceded that anecdotal evidence suggests not all aged care facilities do a good job with palliative and end-of-life care. She, like me, is saddened to hear negative stories like the ones I had heard. Perhaps we just 'got lucky' with the nursing home we chose? We'll never know.

High-quality care should, of course, be a given at all times in the residential aged care sector. By their very nature, nursing homes operate as home hospices, so palliative and end-of-life care should be core business and done well every time. I'm not here to single-out specific organisations, wave political flags or cast blame on state or federal governments for how palliative and end-of-life care is being delivered, but there are clearly some significant systemic issues impacting the aged care sector, both at a community level and within residential facilities, some of which are:

- inadequate levels of resourcing for dementia clients to receive high-quality palliative care, both in the community and within specialist units
- not all aged care staff are adequately trained or supported by their workplaces to deliver high-quality palliative and end-of-life care across the board, never mind for dementia clients
- staff shortages and workforce pressures that present significant ongoing challenges for nursing homes across the board.

In Australia, the Royal Commission into Aged Care Quality and Safety handed down its findings and recommendations in 2021. Its report laid out an extensive plan to overhaul the aged care system and included 148 recommendations. Work is still being undertaken to address the shortfalls identified and implement the recommendations, and it remains very much a work in progress. Watch this space for what this might mean for the aged care sector moving forward.

There are (almost) always choices, though they may not always be obvious

The motivation behind writing this book grew largely out of a desire to get out and about and share our family story. In particular, I wanted to promote choice at the end of life around where, how and with whom to die, choice about interventions and treatment, and choice about what happens post death and how the occasion is recognised (if at all). Although it is not (yet) frequently the case that family members take their relatives out of an aged care facility and move them home to die, I met someone else a few months ago whose family made the same decision as ours, although their dad's move out of his nursing home was much closer to the time of his death than it was for our dad. Like us, for their family it suddenly became very important to have their dad in his familiar home environment as he approached the end of his life. They remain grateful they could achieve this outcome, particularly as his death was during the COVID-19 pandemic when restrictions in aged care facilities were still in place. Advance care planning can have a significant impact on the end of your life – the more prepared you are, the more likely it is you will be able to exercise choice and, subsequently, have your wishes granted.

The key points I want to emphasise in terms of choice are:

You can choose to care for a dying relative at home, if that is consistent with your loved one's wishes

Despite what many people think, you don't have to be a doctor, or have a nursing background, to provide end-of-life care at home, and you don't have to stay in hospital to die, even if that's where you are currently being treated. You also do not need to have a spare bedroom or a second bathroom to create a suitable space in which someone can die peacefully. You do need the right equipment, and the environment certainly needs to be safe but, as it was in our case, your living room will more than suffice if it can be made peaceful and calm for your dying loved one.

If you cannot access government- or community-funded palliative care services – and many people, particularly those with dementia, can't due to ineligibility, long wait times and a lack of resourcing – there are a growing number of private agencies who offer in-home nursing, personal care staff and support workers to assist those who wish to die at home. It might be that more than one agency will support your loved one, something you may be able to coordinate yourself, and it might also be that funding from disability or aged care packages can supplement the cost of some, or all, of that care. Family members can be trained in how to administer medication and provide good quality end-of-life care, or you may wish to engage the services of an end-of-life (or dementia) doula to assist you. What's important is that you choose an agency or individuals who can answer your questions and give you confidence that they will be able to adequately support you and your loved one, both clinically and emotionally. Whoever you choose may be able to assist with equipment or, as it was for us, should be able to refer you to hire services that will have what you need. I won't list the helplines, palliative care services and not-for-profit agencies you may be able to access for advice here, as they differ by location. However, I would encourage you to educate yourself about which services exist in your area, particularly if you wish to die at home or you would like to consider this option for a loved one. I would also urge you to think in advance about your capacity – as a family, or perhaps including a wider network – to care for a dying relative at home and what, if any, limitations there might be on you doing so, such as:

- financial constraints
- work/time pressures
- tasks you wouldn't be comfortable doing
- the amount of time you can sustain care at home
- formulating a Plan B (or even a Plan C) in case caring for a loved one at home becomes too overwhelming and you are unable to cope. It might be that admission to a specialist

palliative care unit/hospice would be an option in that circumstance.

As you read in Chapter 4, being specific with our criteria for when we would bring Dad home (at the point he was bedfast and eating/drinking little) was a key issue for us, and it may well be for you. Asking these questions of yourself is a necessary part of exercising choice and making informed decisions.

You have the choice to change an end-of-life plan if that's what feels right

When Dad entered an aged care facility two years earlier, bringing him back home to die was not on our radar. We assumed he would take his final breaths there. But when that option no longer felt right, we acted to change it to something that did feel right, and we remain SO incredibly thankful we did. It wasn't that we overruled Dad's wishes – we all agreed that he (like the vast majority of others) would have chosen home as a place to die over anywhere else. It had never been our plan to put him into a nursing home in the first place, but Mum's wellbeing was negatively impacted by caring for him at home. It was a 'no-brainer' that he would be comfortable dying at home. As I explained in Chapter 4, it remains my firm belief that Dad wanted to come home and channelled this intention to me so I could make it happen for him. 'The chair of no regret' is a very comfortable chair to sit in, I have to say – if you need to change an end-of-life plan to sit in a chair of no regret, I strongly encourage you to consider doing so. As I indicated above, at least one other family I met that made the same decision as us remains very grateful they did so, with no regrets.

You have the right to enforce your loved one's choices to honour their wishes

Two-thirds of all deaths are expected events – that is, they are not traumatic, accidental or unplanned, and have a clear care trajectory.[13] The overwhelming majority of people who enter residential aged

---

13. Professor Luc Deliens, Palliative Care Queensland Webinar, 17 April 2024

care expect to die in that facility – or in hospital if an illness takes them in that direction – and the vast majority of people affected by chronic health conditions or terminal illness end their days in hospital. Again, that doesn't necessarily mean either of those places must be the final resting place for you or your loved one. However, if the dying person's choice is that a nursing home (as a home hospice) or hospital **is** their preferred place to die, it's still the case they deserve (and indeed should expect) high-quality palliative and end-of-life care. With the exception of unexpected deaths, the majority of considerations for dying patients are, in fact, outside the realm of any medical interventions – in other words, they are more holistic and encompass the social, spiritual, cultural and emotional side of a dignified death. Bearing this in mind, if your loved one plans to die in either residential care or in hospital, be proactive and advocate on their behalf. Ask those services questions such as:

- What are their end-of-life practices, particularly in terms of symptom management and pain relief?
- How often will you be informed of any changes to their condition?
- Who can stay, where would that be and for how long?
- How much involvement will the family be allowed to have with regards to ongoing care?
- How private will the space be?
- Can you play music, dim the lights, bring in children, include pets, have flowers or welcome visitors at any time?
- How long can you sit with your loved one after they have died? Can you assist with washing or preparing the body?

From my own experience, and from what I have read and heard from many others as I have researched this book, the more informed and actively involved those supporting a loved one to die can be, the more likely it is they will find peace and experience a natural bereavement process.

As a society, our levels of 'death literacy' are low

Prior to our experiences with Dad, I can tell you that my own level of death literacy was low. But what does that actually mean? Death literacy is 'the knowledge and skills that make it possible to gain access to, understand and act upon end-of-life and death care options'.[14] It's knowing what good end-of-life care looks like, what happens when someone dies, what legal processes need to be followed, who can be involved, who needs to be notified, what choices there are, what supports are available and so on. We tend to spend a lot of time and energy researching and discussing birthing options when we're expecting a baby (I know I did, at least with our first child!), but somehow we don't prioritise the end of our lives in the same manner, nor talk about death with our loved ones to anything like the same extent.

The message I have received loud and clear, especially over the last twelve months, is that death has become increasingly medicalised, and subsequently institutionalised, and we need to reclaim it as a community issue to feel more empowered. While cultural and social barriers may prevent some people engaging with their loved ones in conversations about death, we really ALL need to do more talking about death and dying in general. We should give particular priority to recording (or at the very least discussing with our loved ones) what our wishes are for the end of our life. There is no minimum age for conversations and documentation around unplanned ill health and death, although it is very easy to consider yourself 'too young' and/or 'too busy' for thinking about such topics until you are forced into doing so. I was guilty of that myself until my parents' mortality became a reality. The simple truth is, the more we embrace these discussions with our family, friends and community members, the more confident we feel in tackling the stigma and taboo that still surround the topic of dying. If we can demystify death, we may be able to alleviate any lingering fears we have about our own death, or the deaths of our loved ones. What's more, if we become increasingly

---

14. https://cbrhl.org.au/what-is-health-literacy/death-literacy/

comfortable discussing our mortality with those closest to us, we will be much better placed to advocate for ourselves, ask questions and talk frankly to our care providers and health staff if/when we are faced with life-changing situations that require us to make decisions. I am so thankful we were able to advocate on Dad's behalf and have honest and open conversations about palliation and life expectancy with his nursing home, particularly when his decline began to accelerate and the end of his life got closer and closer.

Something else I am very grateful for is that our teenagers had the opportunity to be present at their grandad's death. They had grown up with Dad from a young age and walked alongside him as his dementia progressed over the years, so it felt very natural to give them the opportunity to be by his side with Mum, my husband and me as he took his last breath. This is not something we forced them to do – in fact, we gave them both the option to say their goodbyes and then leave if that felt more comfortable. But they didn't, they cried and spoke to Dad just as we did and told us later they were glad they had been there with him until the end. As parents, this was a very comforting thing for us to hear and we felt proud of the decision we had made. I hope this means neither of them will fear death or move into adulthood believing that dying is a taboo subject, a topic people do not wish to discuss. We simply cannot 'reclaim' death and dying as a community issue if we don't get more comfortable talking about it. If people in your family or within your wider network indicate they are open to talking about all things death and dying, start a conversation and encourage everyone to join in! Invite people to explore ideas, consider options, share stories, state their wishes and talk about their concerns. Often, we don't even realise what we are worried about until we start verbalising our thoughts or hear others discussing theirs. Most people won't have completed documentation that records their wishes or even know where to find it. I encourage you to direct them to the links I shared in the previous chapter, or maybe even support them to complete the relevant paperwork if required.

A level of confusion exists about the use of morphine in end-of-life care

As I understand it, being 'ahead of pain' (in other words, good pain management) is one of the key differences between a 'good' and 'not-so-good' death, not only for the dying person but also those around them. Sadly, I have heard and read accounts of loved ones writhing in pain at the end of life (both at home and in residential aged care), suggesting that end-of-life symptoms are not always well managed and understood. Likewise, pain relief is not always adequate. Is this a lack of education around dosage or the right time to administer medication? Is there a lingering perception that prescribing opioids at the end of life will hasten death or be what actually kills the person rather than their underlying illness? Is there also a concern that if opioids are used too early they will create some sort of dependence or build tolerance? With no medical training myself, I am not in a position to explore this issue in any depth, although it is a topic that has been written about extensively. For the purpose of this book, I feel the World Health Organization's fact sheets most simply explain the need for opioids in end-of-life care:

> Pain and difficulty in breathing are two of the most frequent and serious symptoms experienced by patients in need of palliative care. For example, 80% of patients with AIDS or cancer and 67% of patients with cardiovascular disease or chronic obstructive pulmonary disease will experience moderate to severe pain at the end of their lives. Opioids are essential for managing pain.

> Opioids can also alleviate other common distressing physical symptoms including breathlessness. Controlling such symptoms at an early stage is an ethical duty to relieve suffering and to respect a person's dignity.[15]

---

15. https://www.who.int/news-room/fact-sheets/detail/palliative-care

For us, any questions around the use of opioids were answered by either my husband or Kerri-Anne, and both Mum and I felt entirely comfortable with their administration when the appropriate time came to use them. Knowledge is power. If you have questions about what medications will be used at the end of life, including why, when and how they will be administered, ask those questions of the people supporting you. The better informed you are about what to expect when your loved one is dying, the more likely you will find peace and experience a 'normal' grief reaction.

And, finally, what I have learnt about the importance of sharing our palliative dementia story and seeking out the experiences of others

I know Dad would want his family to be happy, even in his absence – he was always an optimist, a glass-half-full kind of guy, who sought out the positives in life. He wouldn't want us to forget about him, never mention his name, never laugh at some of the things he said and did, nor never miss him. But the last thing he would want would be for any of us to be 'stuck' in our grief, feeling guilty about being happy or not embracing all that life still has to offer us. For me, I have realised the power in talking about our experience with Dad – not only because it's a way for me to keep showing him love, which subsequently keeps him alive, but also because sharing our story has the potential to help others and give them confidence to discuss dementia and dying themselves, simply because they know others have.

The grief I have experienced since Dad's death is what is referred to as 'clean' grief. While the loss cuts deep and we miss him every day, the 'wound' heals cleanly and in a healthy manner. This is opposed to 'messy' grief which, as the name suggests, leaves scars, requires complex treatment and may never actually heal. Being with Dad as he died was a profoundly moving and meaningful experience for me and I will be forever grateful I had the opportunity to accompany him into death, alongside Mum, my husband, the kids and even our dog (who always sought out a pat from Dad!). Although the outcome is that Dad is not with us anymore (in person, at least), I feel his death is a 'good news' story that needs to be shared with anyone who is prepared to listen. And my megaphone is at the ready!

Of course, there have been many occasions I have felt incredibly sad I can't visit Dad anymore, bring him home for lunch, take him out for a walk or see him watching us having fun at the beach with our dog. When you love someone, there is an inevitability about the sadness you will feel when they are gone – it's a natural part of the bereavement process. What has brought immense comfort for me since Dad's death has been:

- the incredible power of a living legacy – everything I have done since publishing my first book; sharing our story with the community in various formats/places and now writing a second book – keeps Dad alive for me and provides ongoing motivation to learn more, share more and listen more. The positive impact this drive has had on me is something I struggle to put into words because it's something I feel deep inside my heart

- the security of family life and the warmth of the wider community around us – Mum, my husband, the kids, our friends, the groups we belong to, the activities we participate in and so on

- tapping into the strength of like-minded people who have shared their stories as a means of offering support and comfort to others. Thanks to our connected world, I have read and listened to some truly inspiring individuals. There's much to be gained from 'drinking in' the experiences of others and drawing on their resilience to help you on the days you desperately need it.

TEN

Mum's turn to speak

So far, you've read a lot about me and my focus, feelings and priorities during the last 101 days of Dad's life. Now it feels only fitting to give Mum space to have her say as we come to the final chapter in the book. While we have made all our decisions about Dad's care together and been a huge support for each other, particularly since Dad's dementia diagnosis, Mum's experiences are unique to her and defined by her 60+ year marriage to Dad. Their relationship was challenged by Dad's dementia, the highs and lows of farming over many decades and also Mum's cancer diagnosis and treatment regimen. Just like she did in my previous book, when she laid her innermost feelings bare for all to see, at the age of 83 Mum expresses herself in a raw and vulnerable manner. I am very honoured to share this chapter with you, unabridged and expressed entirely in her own words.

* * *

As I sit down to write the final chapter in this book, I take time to contemplate 'our dementia journey' with Bob. I realise how far we have come since it first started and how much we have learnt and achieved, not only me personally, but all our family. I want to talk now about the last few months of Bob's life and how it affected me, the emotions it evoked and how I was able to cope with those feelings.

I visited Bob most days and took him out regularly, either home for lunch or morning tea or to the beach for a walk, which he always enjoyed. I noticed him becoming more tired and less interested in things. It was also getting harder for him to do certain things now, like holding his eating utensils and directing them to his mouth, which made eating much slower and somewhat frustrating for him. It also became harder for him to get up from a sitting position, with his legs now quite stiff, and he had to use his walker all the time instead of just a walking stick.

As I was observing this, my emotions were all over the place. I felt sadness for him, also for me, and I think at that stage I was somewhat in denial of what I was seeing as I didn't want to face the inevitable decline in Bob. Sometimes I would put on a brave face and say to myself, 'It's okay, he is just having a bad day, he still knows who I am, tomorrow he will be a bit better.' Other days, I would come home crying, either to myself or Lisa, as I struggled to cope with the inevitable changes that were happening. Then he had a fall and was sent to hospital by ambulance, with Lisa and me spending the day there while they did tests and checked him out. Bob was very confused as to why he was there and agitated about what was happening. It was so distressing for him, and distressing for me to see him in such a state. When nothing was broken, they sent him back to his nursing home. It is hard to talk about my emotions at that point – a lot of crying, a lot of soul-searching and also quite a bit of hiding how I was coping from both my family and my friends. Again, I think I was in denial and didn't want to face the grim facts proving that Bob was declining.

As time went on, there were two more unwitnessed falls and one more visit to hospital in the evening, when Bob had a wheezy chest and it was thought he may either have a chest infection or had aspirated. He returned to his care home in the early hours of the morning. After that experience, as a family we said, 'No more hospital.'

After his last fall, Bob went downhill quite quickly. We were now into the bed being down low, a crash mat on the floor and an alarm alert near the bed. It was becoming obvious to me there was going to be quite a change now in Bob's care; he had to be helped out of bed and into a wheelchair; he slept a lot more; he ate a lot less and often had to be helped with eating; he had more pain that had to be dealt with; and he now had to be in a wheelchair, which restricted where we could walk with him. If we could get a wheelchair-modified maxi taxi, we could take him to the beach for a walk, which he still enjoyed. But this was difficult as taxis with wheelchair access are not always available, or you have quite a wait, which isn't suitable when your outing has a time limit.

Throughout this time, we had been thinking a lot about the rest of our family, who live in two other states and were constantly being updated on Bob's condition. We felt perhaps it was time for them to see Bob while he was still able to interact with them. As Lisa was planning the launch of her first book, we decided to have them visit and do the book launch at the same time. This proved to be the right decision, and that whole week with family was great. We saw Bob every day, took him out in his wheelchair to the beach, and he was really good – he knew everyone, and it was very obvious he enjoyed his time, especially with his two sons, who he hadn't seen for a while. For me, that time was bittersweet; I was so pleased to see Bob enjoying his time with everyone, but I remember feeling almost broken when we had to leave him in his nursing home while we all returned to our house together without him. That was really hard. It was good for me to have family around me at that time, as we were all able to talk about Bob and also his condition. That meant we supported each other. We were all feeling sadness, but also gratitude Bob had been so good that week and our visiting family had been able to really interact with him. I remember feeling quite emotional when everyone went home again, I think because I thought that would possibly be the last time they would see Bob. And that brought all my emotions churning around again – sadness, knowing the inevitable was going to happen but not knowing, and not wanting to know, when. There was also a fear of how I was going to handle it when it did.

It was not long after this that Bob's condition began deteriorating quite rapidly, and I could see his quality of life was diminishing. He was sleeping a lot and couldn't get out of bed unless the carers got him up for a shower, but often this was a bed wash. It was about then I realised he may not be with us much longer. I also realised how important it would be for me to tell him about some of the things I wanted to share with him before he got to the stage of possibly not being able to hear or comprehend.

So, I went up the next day and sat with him, told him how much I loved him, what a great life we had had, what a great father and husband he had been and how much his family also loved him. We both cried, but I knew he understood. I also told him not to worry about me, that I would be okay, and our family would be looking out for me. I also felt I wanted him to know we would all be very sad when he was gone, but it was okay because we had all these wonderful memories to share, and he would always be in our hearts. After that, although I was emotionally drained for the first time in a while, I felt at peace within myself. I think this was because I was able to let all my emotions out and tell Bob things I felt were important both for him and me.

Soon after that, Lisa came to me and said she'd had a thought about bringing Bob home, so he could pass away here with family around, and asked what I thought of the idea. My first reaction was 'Would we be allowed to do that?' I didn't think we could – he had been in a nursing home for more than two years. Would they let us? Lisa had been worrying, distraught about her dad maybe passing away and us not being there. What if it was through the night and no one was with him? I had to confess it was something I had struggled over as well, but I had just dismissed it because I thought nothing could be done. Lisa had talked it over with Christian (her husband) and they both agreed it was a great idea, if I was open to it. I was most definitely open to it! When Lisa approached the nursing home, they were very much in support of the idea as well, which I was very grateful for as it made it much easier for us that they were on board.

Everything that we required at home was put in place. The ambulance brought Bob home, and we got him settled into his hospital bed near the window so he could look out at the garden and trees. He was very happy to be home. Daily life went on around him and his needs were looked after by Lisa and Christian around the clock. It meant I could sit with him. We had some of his favourite music on, and it was very relaxed. His grandchildren were involved as well and popped in from time to time. He was never alone and, even when he was sleeping, someone was with him. For me, it was a great relief to have this precious time together without any restrictions or interruptions – just a lovely, calm time. We had Bob home for six days before he passed away very peacefully, his family around him, loving him and giving him permission to go when he was ready.

I couldn't have wished for a better death for Bob. Although I was crying, as we all were when he died, and felt great sadness that my husband of 63 years would no longer be with me, I felt at peace and a great relief he was no longer suffering. I was grateful we had been able to achieve this and enable Bob to pass away at home.

Bob had signed up for the Body Bequest Program, as for years he had wanted to do this. I must admit, when he first said that was what he wanted, I wasn't very keen on the idea. However, I realised this was Bob's decision, so I wouldn't challenge it. We were in touch with the program to let them know we had brought Bob home and that we would be in touch with them again when Bob passed away. I have been very impressed with their approach: the smoothness and the respectful way they handled everything. We had as much time as we required after Bob passed away to just sit with him and talk to one another and grieve. Bob was then collected from the house, and we had a phone call the next day to let us know Bob had arrived at his destination.

On reflection, one of the important things for me at this sad time was that we didn't have to take time, when everyone was grieving, to arrange a funeral. The rest of my family arrived for a week, and we were just able to spend time together. We set our dining table up with lovely Western Australian wildflowers, which Bob had loved, and we had nice food and our 'Bobathon' – we all told our favourite stories about Bob, and there were lots of laughs and cries as we remembered this wonderful husband, father, father-in-law and grandfather. I felt Bob's presence at that time and thought he would be smiling down on us all.

Another nice thing about the Body Bequest Program is that every year they have an 'Thanksgiving and Remembrance Ceremony' for the families of all body donors during the year. We attended the one in March this year. It was beautiful. They had guest speakers, surgeons, paramedics and reflections from a family member whose father was a donor, and they all spoke about how the program had helped them in their jobs. The thing that struck me the most was how respectful everyone was, and how grateful they were towards the families of the donors. When the time comes, Bob will be cremated, and we will be given his ashes. We will then, as a family, take them to Bob's final resting place in accordance with his wishes.

I miss Bob in my heart every day, but I very much feel at peace within myself. I believe this is because we were able to bring Bob home, be with him at the end of his life and know that he knew he had been very much loved. Some days, I believe I can almost feel his presence and he is smiling, which gives me great comfort.

Before I finish my chapter, I want to mention how much gratitude and love I have for Lisa and Christian, as they were the ones who nursed Bob with such care and respect. Without them, this may not have happened, as I would not have thought it possible. I have since learnt that taking someone out of a nursing home and returning them home to die is certainly possible, and there is help available for anyone who would like to do this – I would certainly recommend it. To all my wonderful family who have held me close and comforted and supported me through this difficult time, thank you. I love you all dearly.

In closing, one other thing that has come out of this experience for me is that I am now signing up to the same Body Bequest Program as Bob. After seeing how it works, and the way in which it helps our medical professionals in their very important work, I cannot think of a more fitting way to contribute.

* * *

And there you have it. In her own words, that is Mum's very personal account of how the last few months of Dad's life felt for her, and the peace his death has delivered. What a gift. Reading her beautiful sentiments has brought tears to my eyes every single time I have done so – tears of love, tears of pride and tears of gratitude. Like me, Mum hopes her words will bring comfort to others and inspire them to seek out choices about the end of a loved one's life, particularly if they want to exercise more control than they may be currently feeling.

Conclusion

Now that you have reached the end of the book, I assume the rationale behind the title I chose has become clear to you. We found peace immediately after Dad's death, and that has been a tremendous gift for all of us – Mum, me, the kids, my husband and my brothers. My husband never got the opportunity to provide care for his own dad at the end of his life as he was on the other side of the world, so he feels his role in 'cradling' Dad into death was just as honouring and gratifying for him as it was for me. He saw it as a nice way to 'pay Dad back' for some of the many things he has done for him/us over the years – not that Dad ever kept score, of course. Similarly, for my brothers, knowing Dad was in his home environment and cared for by us as he calmly took his last breath was hugely comforting. Once again, a gift.

But the gift was not only for those of us left behind. We know a peaceful death also delivered a gift for Dad – he was at home, comfortable and pain-free, surrounded by love and reassuring, familiar voices. I'm very sure his soul was happy as it left his physical body on the day he died. And that is the gift a good death can deliver. Peace at the end of life.

Could others do what we did?

Of course. People die at home every year, supported by private nursing staff, family carers, community services, doulas or specialist palliative care teams. In that sense, we are no different to thousands of other families who have chosen a home death for their loved one, and that's exactly what the concept of building compassionate communities is about – increasing death literacy and widening the reach of palliative and end-of-life care so communities can confidently support their own members when they are dying.

It's true that I am a social worker, and my husband is a nurse practitioner, but our motivation to take Dad out of an aged care facility and facilitate his death at home came from a position of love for him, not as a result of our professional backgrounds. It would be arrogant to suggest our job titles were completely irrelevant in the whole scenario, because they weren't – obviously we both have relevant skills and we drew on those throughout the process. And, in the absence of any funding being available for Dad, our family also had the means to pay for private staff as needed, so this was not a consideration as it may be for others. However, having said all that, it would be totally inaccurate to assume everyone needs a certain job title to provide their loved one with high-quality palliative and end-of-life care. That has been proven wrong many, many times over and will continue to be disproven. With support, we know the pathway we took is one that could be reproduced by others, **if that was the wish and preferred choice of the person dying.** Once again, the need for ongoing education, additional resources and better-connected communities is vital as our population ages.

What were the most important factors in us being able to do what we did?

I believe these are the key points in our story that ultimately ensured the choices we made delivered a positive outcome for all of us. Even if you are not planning a home death or taking someone out of a nursing home, I think they are worth a quick recap:

- We engaged with the **advance care planning process** as soon as Dad was diagnosed with dementia, and we had a clear idea of his wishes, beliefs and value base.

- We were a **proactive family** who kept a close clinical eye on where Dad was at and sought advice about his life expectancy as his condition deteriorated.

- We always maintained open dialogue and a **good relationship with the nursing home**, which proved invaluable when it came to a discussion about transferring Dad home and getting the timing right to do so.

- We felt **confident** changing the end-of-life plan when it no longer felt like the right one.

- We accessed palliative-specific support to oversee the care at home process, could ensure a safe environment and were **well prepared**, both practically and emotionally.

- We had a **willingness** to do whatever it took, in the best way we could, to provide Dad with what we thought would be his preference for his final days. It was our firm belief that no one loved him as much as his family, therefore no one could provide more loving care than we could.

- We had **capacity**, with my husband using long service leave and me taking time away from work.

- We created **time**, shutting off other areas of our lives to prioritise Dad, be in the moment with him and allow space for the end of his life to play out.

It's about choice

There's not one model of end-of-life care that constitutes good practice to the exclusion of all others. However, there is the ability for families to tailor what they have, what they want and how they can get it. **It's about choice.** People want choices and to know what all their options are, regardless of where their preferred place of death might be. Dying at home does not appeal to everyone, and it would be foolish to suggest all families should feel compelled to make death at home a reality for their loved one – that would be farcical and would, in fact, go **against** all concepts of personalised care and individualised decision-making. But what I hope I have been able to demonstrate is that the path we took may be an option for others, **if that is their choice.**

In closing

I remain grateful to whatever it was that forced me to look at the previously assumed place of death for Dad and decide to completely change it, and how the whole process panned out for our family. To be honest, it's almost irrelevant how, or even why, we changed the plan. The most important thing is that we realised we had a choice and decided to exercise that choice to create the most peaceful death we could for Dad. As a family, I firmly believe we got it right.

I'm certain Dad would be so proud, and so happy, to know the experiences we have had with him, especially in the latter years of his life, are driving us to start conversations about dementia and dying well, talk about subjects people often find taboo, increase our own knowledge base and support others. What a wonderful legacy for a great man. For me personally, the passion that has developed in me to share our story as widely as possible is exciting. I am looking forwards to seeing where the future might take me.

Detailing our family story, explaining the choices we made and 'doing my bit' to help educate people and create compassionate

communities were the motivations behind writing this book. I hope you have enjoyed reading our palliative dementia story as much as I have enjoyed writing it.

Get in touch with Lisa

Website: www.lisatwigg.com

Email: lisa@eightyyearswithoutdementia.com

Facebook: Eighty Years Without Dementia

Acknowledgments

First and foremost, I want to acknowledge Mum's contribution to this book – not only that she was comfortable with me spelling out (in a lot of detail) what the last few months of Dad's life looked like for us as a family, but also for her agreeing to write the final chapter. Initially, she was a bit concerned about that, worried she might not 'get it right' or 'do it well enough'. I told her just to write from the heart, and I'm sure you would agree that's exactly what she did. I would never have pursued the idea of bringing Dad home to die if Mum had not been immediately supportive, and I will be forever grateful she was.

To Kerri-Anne, thank you from the bottom of my heart. Not only did you give me the confidence to do something unconventional, and then assisted our family to achieve a good death for Dad, but your encouragement to write this book, and your contribution to it, has been invaluable. I'm deeply grateful for your time and input.

To Kathy, another bottom-of-my-heart thank you – for the (many) conversations, the sharing of stories, the proofread and detailed feedback, and the ongoing encouragement. I'm so glad you are in my corner and I hope you stay there for a very long time.

To Leah, I'm so appreciative our paths have crossed! Thank you for taking an interest in this book, offering your support and agreeing to write the foreword. You're doing such important work in the dementia space, and I look forwards to many more breakfast 'meetings'.

To Kerry, Annette, Louise, Ann, Nicolle and Jacqui – I could not have put our own experience into any kind of context without your thoughts, wisdom and ideas. Big thanks to all of you for sharing your firsthand experiences with me so freely and willingly.

To Rebecca and Kirsty, thank you for embracing this project and helping me send it out into the world. Not only do you understand the importance of the subject matter, you also show the utmost respect for the voice of the storyteller. I'm so glad I found you.

To my older brothers, as I say in the book, your support has always been unwavering and it has made the journey with Dad so much easier to navigate – the phone calls, the messages, the encouragement, the thanks, the trust, the visits and the maintaining of a connection with both Mum and Dad, despite the geographical distance between us. It's been a team effort, and I consider myself extremely lucky to have you both as siblings.

And finally, to my beloved hubby, Christian – your support for me writing this book was always without question, but what is even more important is the monumental role you played in the story. You always cared for Dad in the most beautiful, respectful way, but you went above and beyond when it came to bringing him home to die. Although I have said it to you many times, I doubt you will ever fully understand how grateful I am for the love you showed Dad, and subsequently the rest of our family, at the end of his life. As you know very well, I love you beyond Chiron x

About the author

Lisa Twigg is an independent social worker. During her career, Lisa has worked in both inpatient and community mental health settings, sexual assault crisis services, child protection, foster care and emergency medicine. Along the way, she has taken time away from her career to have children, home educate and undertake home-based support work for NDIS-funded clients. However, Lisa's motivation to share the story of her dad's 'good death' stems purely from her role as a 'daughter'. Having made the unconventional decision to take their dad Bob out of residential care and bring him home to die, Lisa and her family are keen to inspire others by talking about, and promoting, choice at the end of life.

Lisa lives in Greater Brisbane with her husband, two children and their pet Jack Russell. Lisa's mum, Helen, lives in a granny flat under their family home.